Jerry

a friend & fellow teacher.

Someone who has put up

In the Image of God

with many meditative

conversations over dinner.

Hope you enjoy

the book

Daniel [illegible]

By Daniel J. Shepard:

You & I Together: Have a Purpose in Reality
Reality and Existence

In thc Image of God:
Free Will and Determinism

Forthcoming Title:
Knowledge and Prophecy

In the Image of God

Free Will and Determinism

Daniel J. Shepard

Proctor Publications

Published in the USA by
Proctor Publications
PO Box 2498, Ann Arbor, MI 48106

Library of Congress Catalog Number: 97–66237

Publisher's Cataloging in Publication
(Prepared by Quality Books)
Shepard, Daniel J., 1945–
In the Image of God: Free Will and Determinism
by Daniel J. Shepard.
p. cm.
ISBN: 1–882792–41–6

1. Panentheism. 2. Free will and determinism. I. Title

BT98.S44 1997 211'.2
QBI97–40445

Preface

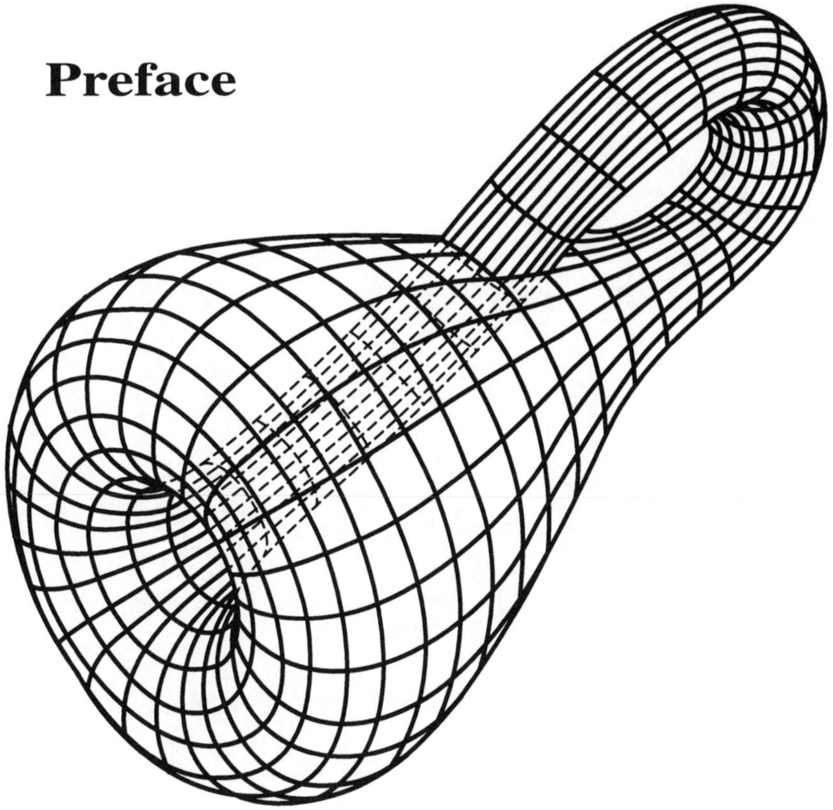

The Klein Bottle

For something or someone on the *outside*, there appears to be nothing *inside*, for there appears to be no *inside*. For something or someone on the *inside*, the bottle, vessel, is filled with violence, pain, and trauma inflicted on each and every entity confined within its far distant walls. Pain, subjugation, intimidation, greed, injustice, and abuse are spinning out of control, driving unchecked through time because the objects – entities – within do not understand.

To Begin

1996 A.D.: Where do we begin? We begin with truth, as revolting as it may seem. The place? The most technologically advanced country in the world, the epicenter of humankind's quest to protect the species' vulnerability to annihilation via global cataclysmic events perpetuated by nature and by humankind itself.

The action? Two 18-year-old teenagers, one male, one female, prepare to eliminate a crisis hanging over their lives. The crisis? A life altering event, the introduction of a life into the world, a life that would cause a commitment, a life-style change of major impact upon two young lives – a change neither teen is ready to accept.

In a small room in a little motel in Delaware, two youngsters journey their dark hours together. In their minds, the waters they must maneuver are so black they must confide in no one. They have only each other, soul mates, in which to confide. Their passage is so bleak, so sinister, it is as if they are navigating the muddy waters of morality by the light of a moonless night. The only source they have to guide them comes from three stars high overhead: the star of social law, the star of faith, and the star of logic.

The young girl is quietly crying. He is holding her as they wait for the "beautiful" event to happen. She experiences the fear of a life filled with possible pain from social rejection and parental disapproval over an event that will control and consume her life. This event will remove any control she feels she has over her life's journey. Emotions coming in sharp cascading undulations of regularity rack her mind with pain greater than the pain of the labor. He holds her with trembling hands as he tries to reassure her, comfort her, comfort himself. He empathizes with her emotional pain while fearing her physical pain. Inundated with fear and confusion, she looks inward for a sense of direction but sees only the muddied waters within an eddy of contradicting principles.

Between the pain of contractions, they each gaze inward, desperately searching the imaginary heavens of their minds for the light. The only emanating lights come from three stars.

Star one – social morality as defined by social laws:

The brightest light, the closest light, the most promising light emanates from the star of social law and social institutions. The message is clear. The local radio stations have broadcast the information for a year. The local TV stations have painted the visual pictures for all to see. The local papers have been a battleground for the controversial debate. The public schools have used the concept as an exciting source of debatable material for their youngsters. Regardless of the general trend in public opinion, the fact remains that society had made a commitment.

Two youngsters, eighteen years young, saw what they perceived to be society's decision, society's final decree through the sacredness of the law itself. The decree: a fetus is not a viable entity. Society has clearly declared that it is okay to intrude on the inner sanctum of the woman's body and physically turn the fetus at nine months in order to force it to emerge feet first. The purpose: to stop the birthing process at the point when the feet, body, shoulders, and neck emerge into what should be its reality for the next 90 years, a reality to which it was sent for a reason.

A nurse holds the red, wet, helpless body while the head is forced to stay within the birthing canal. A doctor, a protector of life, drives scissors into the base of the skull, into the brain itself. The point is not to kill the fetus, but rather to open a hole, a small hole with a sinister purpose. Methodically, the protector of life takes a small tube and prepares to insert it into the hole created in the skull.

The fetus struggles in the hands of the nurse, the comforter of the sick. With its head held in the warmth of the birthing canal, the fetus listens to the reassuring heartbeat of its mother, the sound it has always known, always took comfort in. The fetus is overwhelmed with the warmth of its mother against its head, the strength of forceful hands around its body, the coldness of steel penetrating its neck, and the pain of the world surging through its skull.

Then, with all the skill of a trained professional, the protector of life methodically inserts a small tube into the "expertly" created incision. Reaching over, he turns on a machine and the brain is slowly sucked out of the "unborn fetus." The journey is terminated.

The starlight the two youngsters see emanates from society, a society that says that sucking out a fetus' brain seconds before birth is okay, that says capital punishment – murder – is okay. They see a society that says a man who viciously rapes women and children needs only serve a few years in prison in order to fully pay his debt to society. They see a society that tells the same man that if he behaves in prison, they will absolve him of part of his debt.

The starlight of morality emanating from the star of social morality proves confusing. Add a little rationality from an 18-year-old brain and all of a sudden it is just as moral to terminate the fetus' life four minutes after birth as at birth as long as it is done quickly. The 18-year-old brain asks, "Does four minutes make anymore of a logical difference as to when taking a life is moral or immoral?" Continuing with the semi-sophisticated logic of an 18-year-old, if one offsets the time of four minutes with a less traumatic, less inhumane means of dying, then the two should balance each other. The method in mind is a quick blow to the head and then simple suffocation in a trash bag, a dark environment similar to the one the fetus has experienced during its total existence.

But society disagrees with the rationality of the two youngsters and has built into its laws a technicality. Delaware law requires prosecutors to seek the death penalty for the "murder of any person under fourteen years of age." Using a technicality in the law and the social outline of morality, Delaware will pompously make a decision to either kill the two teenagers or ignore its own laws. All the while Delaware debates its decision, the two teenagers huddle in fear for their own lives and shame for what they did to a living entity, an action they believed to be more humane and less traumatic than that of a doctor during partial birth abortion.

Their crime involved rationalizing a decision they had to make using the starlight of society as a guide. We are all forced to follow this starlight; if we do not, we will surely suffer the consequences of our actions.

Star two – religious morality as defined by faith:

Having barely begun their journey in life, the two frightened youngsters are confused and dazed by the intense starlight of social morality, social law, as it fades into the blackness of the heavens only to be replaced by the self-righteous light generated by the star of religious morality. The starlight radiates its message with the force of indignation, beaming down from the star of compassion, the star of religious morality – faith:

"It is very clear that it is not moral to take the life of a living entity. It's the law of God. Everyone knows it. There is no excuse for not understanding the simplicity of it. You are eighteen and should know better. How would you like to have someone kill your mother, father, brother, sister or, for that matter, you? What would become of society if we tolerated murder? Therefore, we feel it is only right that you suffer the consequences of your action.

"We, therefore, are going to sentence you to death. No, this is not murder; this is something that needs to be done to make an example of you so others will not also take the heinous action you performed upon that poor innocent child. No, we will not be inhumane and we will be merciful by choosing a non-traumatic method of termination for you. We will use lethal injection rather than suffocate you in a bag as you did to your innocent baby. You will not be terminated through the process of having your brain sucked out by means of a small tube inserted through a hole punctured into the base of your skull, as is performed in partial birth abortion allowed under Delaware law. That is inhumane and we could never allow such action to be directed toward you.

"We have listened to your excuse for committing such an abhorrent act. We understand your logic of following the starlight of social morality and law. We do not accept your decision to add some sense of rationality to that law because it goes against morality, religious morality. Have you no faith?!

"Your sentence is now pronounced. You are to die for your actions. We are going to kill you in the name of justice, in the name of morality, a morality that transcends social morals. We are going to kill you because you killed and killing is wrong. The means of death: lethal injection, and may God have mercy upon your souls."

Whose soul needs the mercy of God? Yours and mine, for we are a part of this society. We are a part of this confusion. We are a part of this constant state of moral confusion and chaos.

Why did the two eighteen-year-olds terminate the journey of

their newborn? Does it matter? Whatever the reason, the starlight of faith was not enough. Whether they chose to follow the light of social reason because it served their own ends or because they really believed in the established social morals and laws is not important. What is important is that social and personal conflict and confusion will continue to exist unless we find a means of resolving our moral conflicts.

Star three – a universal philosophy and universal morality defining reality and our purpose within it:

The solution comes from star three, a distant star so far away, its light is barely discernible. But we have the tools, the technology, the rationality to focus in on that star and magnify its significance. We have the ability to begin the initial, in-depth study of star three in earnest. We can understand.

The message from this star is clear. Reality has a purpose, you are in reality, you have a purpose in reality. No one has the right to terminate anyone's journey for any reason. The message is simple, clear, uncomplicated. The implications are simple, clear, uncomplicated. The message emanates not from the star of social morals and social laws and not from the star of religions and faith. The message emanates from a star of logic, a star of philosophy, a star with the message of a universal philosophy. The star's name is panentheism. It is not a religion. It is a philosophy. Religion is a subject of faith. Philosophy is a subject of reason.

The star is far away from our thoughts because the light is very dim in its infancy; the star is nothing more than a fetus. Our understanding of who we are in reality has moved through the primeval period, animism, polytheism, henotheism, theism, pantheism, and is now coming to the panentheism stage. Panentheism is a message from a star that says all humans are created equally; we are all equal for our essence is our souls, not our bodies or minds. The soul comes from outside this reality through which it travels, and is located within its Creator. The soul journeys this reality to increase the very magnificence of the Creator. What is the soul? The soul is none other than a piece of the Creator Itself. In other words, the soul is, in essence, God.

If the star had been older and if the star had been embraced by society and religions, what then? Then two youngsters would have been sitting in a small motel room in Delaware, holding an infant, and seeing a piece of God, and that would have made all the difference.

Only Words

Speculation 2000 A.D.: WWIII, Roe vs. Wade, continues. This is a war of phenomenal proportions and magnitude that is not recognized as a war. It is a war defining the "beginning" and the "end" of each person's journey through life. It splits families, reeks emotional personal havoc, scars young and old alike, and takes countless lives. It has been going on for over thirty years, laying siege to our very souls. Ironically, we don't even see it for what it is. We don't understand it is a war because we don't even know what the war is about.

The war is over the definition of life. When does life begin and when does it end? Actually, the war is not only over a definition of when life begins and ends, but rather a statement of philosophy, a philosophical perception of what life is. If we do not understand what life is, we cannot define when it begins or ends. The struggle continues over the right to control one's body, the right to die with dignity, the rights of the unborn, the rights of the father, the right to one's privacy and the right to life.

The concept of who has the right to terminate the journey of another centers around two fundamental definitions: that of life and of death. This is not an insignificant exercise. This is one of the most crucial battles in our history. This affects every man, woman, and child alive today and who will be alive in the future.

The conflict taking place is not just a conflict; it is a war. World War II had fifty million casualties. This war has had far more than that already and isn't close to being over. It involves religious institutions, governmental institutions, political groups, social groups, activists on both sides, and pacifists in the middle. It involves millions of people banding together to wage the war. It involves the fundamental moralities of our future societies. This is a war of desperation, a war of principle, a war to protect one's own journey, a war to protect the journey of others. This is a war in which members of both sides can be proud to have participated. This is a global war, having extremely large casualty counts, inflicting extreme pain and suffering both physically and emotionally upon unbelievable numbers of people, and pulling every aspect of almost all cultures into the fray worldwide. This is certainly World War III.

The war is essentially over two words, "life" and "death," and what we find acceptable in terms of their definition. The war is as legitimate and noble a war we, as a species, have ever engaged in. This is a war over the very definition of who we as a species and as individuals perceive ourselves to be. The two words, life and death, are key to our perception of our very existence within reality.

The results of this war, WWIII, will set the ambiance of our social and environmental reality well into the future of humankind. The repercussions of the war will affect our perception of ourselves and our species well into the next millennium and possibly beyond. In fact, the outcome of the war could very possibly determine the survival of our species.

The war has been taking place for over three decades. The end is not in sight. What will end the war? Nothing we presently have in place within society. The element needed to end the war and resolve the issue in an acceptable manner to all sides is missing. We are missing an acceptable perception of what reality is, who we are as a people and as individuals, and what our purpose is within this reality. Understanding what reality is and what our purpose is within reality would lead us to an acceptable consensus regarding what life is and what death is, which would end the war.

How we define "life" and "death" will define what we perceive ourselves and our function in reality to be. This is thinking backward and that is why the war still rages and no solution is appearing on the horizon, in spite of over thirty years of conflict and pain. Actually, the words of the above statement are correct but they are not in the correct order. The statement should be, *How we define ourselves and our function in reality will define what we perceive "life" and "death" to be.*

Let's first attempt to approach the war from the aspect of the first statement. The most logical place to begin would be to look in a respected philosophy dictionary. It is interesting that both R. Audi's *The Cambridge Dictionary of Philosophy* and W. Reese's *Dictionary of Philosophy and Religion* contain over 4,000 entries each and over 850 pages each, but neither reference defines "life," "alive," "death" or "dead" (interesting omissions considering the significance of the terms in relationship to our existence within reality).

We accept the termination of existence within this reality as death and we accept existence within this reality as "life." These two statements, however, are not going to be adequate definitions for the general population, let alone academia. Let's look at each term individually to help reveal acceptable definitions.

Death

The first place to start should probably be "death." Although this has accelerated into an explosive issue, it is nevertheless the least explosive of the two social issues. It is also, oddly enough, a key to defining life. If we can agree upon what death is, we may be able to resolve the issue of life.

Webster's Dictionary states that death is "a permanent cessation of all vital functions: the end of life." The definition, "the end of life" isn't going to help since we are starting with "death" and have not yet defined "life." So we will have to explore the definition, "a permanent cessation of all vital functions." Fortunately, the definition of "death" has already been put in place by medical ethics boards composed of doctors, religious leaders from various religious backgrounds, laymen, etc.

Originally, death was thought to mean the cessation of breathing. If no breath was emanating from the body for a period of time, death was formally declared. Today, we know people can go into comatose states where breathing is almost impossible to detect without proper equipment. We know people can be submerged for long periods in icy water and be revived with no mental dysfunction. We can, with medicine's new technology, also disconnect people from their lungs and keep them healthy for long periods of time using heart lung machines. Other people can be kept alive without the use of their "vital" organs, i.e. the kidneys. Even half the brain can now be removed without death or total incapacitation.

Because of these advances, the medical ethics committees had to create a different definition of "death." They moved to what laymen would term "flat-lined brain waves" on an EEG, electroencephalograph. Religions, doctors, lawyers, society, the general public, fathers, mothers, sons, daughters, government – almost everyone accepts this as a time of "death" or, in other words, a time when one's journey in life has ended. When a flat-lined brain wave signal shows up on an EEG, everyone accepts the concept of pulling the plug on any life support systems the patient may be relying upon to keep their "vital" organs functioning. It took us a while to accept this definition of "death," but it is now almost universally accepted.

We then need to step into the violent fray of defining "life."

Life

With "death" defined as the termination of brain waves by the brain, the definition of "life" should logically flow into place as the initiation of the production of brain waves. This occurs at a specific time in the development of the fetus. It doesn't start at birth and it doesn't start at conception.

This definition of "life" is not going to please either side in the war we are experiencing, but in terms of logic, it is going to be difficult to refute since it is based on the opposite of society's definition of "death." The definition is one developed by medical ethics committees in their attempt to diffuse the issue of what to do with brain-dead patients that medicine was capable of keeping alive for decades. The definition of "death" is a definition that society generally recognizes and accepts. Society also accepts the concept that the opposite of "death" is "life" and thus the logical definition: "life" begins when the brain starts emitting brain waves, when the brain becomes a viable organ, when the brain begins to function.

If we accept this definition for life, then the solution to many problems becomes simplistic and acceptable to the general public as well as to academia. The result: the war over abortion and capital punishment finally ends with little more than a sigh. The war is actually defined out of existence. There will still be discussion and dissension, but for the most part, heated conflicts based on "principle" will have had the wind taken out of their sails.

What if we approach the issue from a more philosophical standpoint? What if we approach the issue from the direction of first defining who we are in reality and what our function in reality is and then tackle the issues of "life" and "death?" Will the outcome still be the same? To find out, let's attempt to approach the war from the aspect of the second statement, How we define ourselves and our function in reality, will define what we perceive "life" and "death" to be. Surprisingly, it will lead us to the same solution, just more emphatically.

Philosophy

Theism basically states that God and reality are separate entities and, therefore, that humans and God are separate entities. Pantheism basically states that God and reality are the same and thus humans are not separate from God, that humans are a portion of God. Neither philosophy has been able to bring solution to the issues. Quite the contrary. One has only increased a state of pacifism towards the issue and the other has only added fuel to the fire. If we take the best of both philosophies and accept the theism concept that God is larger than reality, and add to this the concept of pantheism that God and reality are important to each other, you have basically panentheism. Panentheism adds the concept that reality is not separate from God but contained within God, and that although God may be all knowing, all powerful, and all present, It becomes even more so by journeying reality.

Acceptance of this philosophy does nothing to destroy religions. All significant religions are built on a philosophy of theism or pantheism. To broaden their philosophy base significantly enough to incorporate panentheism does not alter their credibility. What it does, however, is make room for a rational understanding and acceptance of the definition of "death" put forward by medical ethics committees. And with this definition, a panentheistic philosophical base opens religions up to accepting a definition of "life" that coincides with the definition of "death."

How does this all come about? A panentheistic philosophy would argue that God travels what we call reality through the machine of humans and other intelligent life forms. When the machine is no longer viable, God's journey, our journey in reality, is over. Our soul, God, leaves the body. Lack of brain activity indicates the end of the journey, at which point a person is proclaimed "dead."

When the machine is viable, God's journey, our journey in reality, begins. Our soul, God, enters the body. The indication of the start of this journey is the beginning of brain activity, at which point a person is proclaimed "alive."

Panentheism produces the same result. The war finally ends with little more than a sigh. The war is actually defined out of existence through having defined what the essence of an individual is within reality and what the function of an individual is within reality. This result may be the same as the previous process but it is much more significant, for it manages to establish our identity and purpose in reality in understandable terms. It establishes what reality itself is in an understandable fashion, while at the same time reinforcing our religions, cultures, and traditions. In addition, it would not only end the war, but would also end many perplexing problems we have faced and that we will face in the future concerning controversial issues such as capital punishment, abortion of a fetus after brain function begins, use of early development fetal material for medical research, use of the placenta for medical purposes, growth of fetal tissue for the purpose of producing organs for organ transplants, acceptance of organs grown from early fetal tissue, abortion of early development fetal tissue caused by rape or incest, termination of a patient not on life support systems whose brain is still functioning, and on it goes. . .

Who will "win" and who will "lose" with a universal acceptance of this definition of "life" and "death?" The winners will be on both sides of the battle:

- Fathers who want a say in the life and death decisions of their offspring.
- Women who want control over their bodies.
- Couples who want to determine if a raped wife is pregnant with the husband's child.
- Souls who would have had the potential to journey through life.
- Society that may lose a "pillar" of strength or creativity.
- Unbending parents whose religions would deny their children the mercy of abortion after being subjected to rape or incest.
- The judicial system as it attempts to rationalize partial birth abortion.

- Religious organizations that wrestle with moral conflicts within their membership.
- Abortion clinic employees wrestling with the conflict of "right" and "wrong," what's best for the mother to be, what's best for the infant to be.
- Political parties presently lined up on each side of the issue of abortion or capital punishment, etc.

The losers will be potential life, fetal material before the brain starts to function. If potentiality, however, is one's definition of "life," then one needs to go much further than protecting the fetal tissue in its primary stage. With potentiality for life as the definition of "life," one would need to prohibit any form of birth control ranging from the withdrawal method to vasectomy, since any act of sexual union would have "potential" for life. Society, religions, and government would have their work cut out for them. Intrusion into the privacy of the home, not to mention the bedroom, would be all pervasive.

The alternative: define "death," "life," "killing," and "murder" in ways that are most expedient for our own self interests, our politics, our religions, our particular social setting. The problem is that by generating definitions as basic as these on the foundation of expediency allows the generation of other definitions on the same bases. Definitions based upon expediency rather than universal rationality leads to dangerous situations such as infanticide, genocide, racism, genderism, sexism, bigotry, etc.

It is your choice and my choice. We can end World War III or we can live life as usual and extend the war indefinitely. History indicates we will not be ready to take the simple step of ending violence and conflict. It may be the year 2000 A.D., but we will not be ready to take the small step of redefining our perception of ourselves, the step up to a different status and position of responsibility within reality. Instead, a new war is about to break out in 2050.

The Choice

Speculation 2050 A.D.: Social ambiance becomes a major crisis for humankind and, as in the case of WWIII, humankind isn't even aware of it being a problem. What innocent and unaware creatures we are.

Social scientists begin to look at the overall picture regarding the ambiance of society as a whole. Civil and social engineers begin to consciously culture the established social atmosphere. They begin to acknowledge that wherever people are or have been, we leave behind a type of scent or presence that is almost impossible to eliminate. Once people have visited, our presence always lingers. Sometimes we like passing through what people before us have set in place and sometimes we abhor it. It exists in homes, religious centers, governmental institutions, cities, recreational settings, whole nations, entire continents, our total planet, and space itself

Social engineers begin studying the scent of humankind, the feel one obtains, the atmosphere that one becomes immersed within and surrounded by as one moves in and out of a particular environment touched by people. Some environmental ambiances give a sense of compassion, love, awe, warmth, trust, security, happiness. Other ambiances give a sense of fear, anxiety, insecurity, depression, sadness, paranoia.

Social scientists and engineers do not fully comprehend that we can all "improve" our behaviors. The leaders in power feel they know best, are above others, and have no need to improve. Change in behavior, however, only comes about with a change in a perception of ourselves. To elevate the behavior of everyone from the most socially abhorrent to the most socially idealistic would require a change in perception in reality, a change in the perception of our purpose in reality, a change for all at the same time.

Social engineers at the bottom of corporations designing new social plans are unable to persuade their superiors of the need to change the basic perceptions we have of each other. Fundamental and dramatic social change is not what the powers to be nor those holding power presently have in mind. In fact, rather than the replacement of status and power, the main design being developed intends to consolidate and amplify the status and power of those already in high places.

The elite have made their choice and it is more of the same. Their choice is to continue a sterile, cold, calculating, judgmental, and guilt-ridden society, while at the same time perpetuating an aura of fear and anxiety towards moving on to the next journey. It initiates a sense that the next journey, the journey after life, will be no better than this journey and will probably be even more intense in its inhumane aura.

Society accepts the direction provided by social engineers, scientists, politicians, intellectuals, economically elite, religious institutions, and governmental agencies. Society has, through its leadership, chosen. Society chose to maintain that people and God are separate entities. God is greater than us; we are subservient to God; we have no real significance other than in reality. Therefore, once we are no longer able to contribute constructively to society, we have the obligation to terminate our existence so the resources of society may be directed to those that are productive.

Throughout society arise countless warm, compassionate places for nonproductive people to terminate their existence. The depressed, the suicidal, the differently abled, the disfigured, the elderly, the loners, and the "leaches" on society all have a place to which they can retire. Warm nurturing places are available to all seeking an acceptance of their decision to move on to a new journey. All children have been oriented and educated in the culture of social efficiency. They will never fear doing what is best for society when they are no longer productive. Death is truly a righteous and moral act to take by those truly concerned with others and society. Leaders in power have done much to improve society, but nothing can compare to the conveniently located termination centers.

Social ambiance has become a respected field of study and has gained respect through its success in maintaining the perception that people are lowly creatures, servants of another, servants of God, animals on a level below God. Status levels are being fine-tuned to the ultimate degree, even to that existing between people and God.

This is truly a monumental moment in time for humankind. It is a time sealed by history itself. Simultaneous with the formal celebration of the establishment of a new socially engineered ambiance, a small group of the most prominent panentheistic thinkers, comprising the heart of a little noticed back room think-tank, are rounded up in the dark of night and are whisked away to some quiet unknown destination. Transported with them are documents containing the basic concepts and social designs they have generated, which they believed would lead to massive change within society – a change starting at the very foundation of the perception we have regarding the purpose of life. Although these people would never be seen or heard from again, one item confirming the presence of their journey in reality was overlooked. A few paragraphs from some personal papers were left to drift with the winds.

. . .and so ambiance in an environment is established by people based upon their perception of who they are. When people think too small, too little of themselves, and feel they have no purpose in reality, in society, they often act in ways to satisfy their own personal short-term yearnings. "What do I want, what can I do now, at this very moment, to make myself feel good?" With sensory hedonism, the process of obtaining personal pleasure through sight, smell, touch, hearing, and taste can become so intense that out come uncontrolled animalistic behavior such as rape, vengeance, power play, intimidation.

When people expand their thoughts and concepts of themselves, feeling their purpose in reality, in society, they move from personal short-term goals to personal long-term goals. Long-term goals orient around spiritual needs, needs of the soul, people's essence or what might better be called spiritual hedonism. A spiritual orientation leads to questions such as, "What do I want out of life? What can I do now to obtain my long-term goals, to make myself feel satisfied with my life's journey even when I am about to face death? How do I maximize my journey through eternity? What must I face after death?"

When people have small conceptions of themselves, feeling no purpose in reality or society, they act erratically and detrimentally to others, what one would call "animalistic." The random and bewildering behaviors of murder, rape, theft, intimidation, power play, abuse, infanticide, and suicide are active and passive violence committed by people against not only others but even to themselves. Violence continually surfaces in society as people react to their status of inferiority to God.

Ironically, as the concept of the significance people have of themselves increases, so does the damage they do to others. There is, however, an interesting point where this acceleration suddenly shatters and is instantly replaced by a whole new behavior pattern oriented around eternity rather than the time span of mortals. Those thinking in terms of today do damage today. Those thinking globally up to the time of their mortal termination do global damage, i.e. Hitler. Their thoughts seldom remain at a level beyond mortality, however. Their thoughts range from now to the end of their mortal existence. People who have an expanded conception of themselves, feeling purpose in eternity and in touch with existence beyond mortality, act in a different manner than those with short-term visions. Long range visions extend from now, past the time of death, into eternity itself. The further into eternity people think, the more compassionate they become, the more idealistic their ideas emerge. Both types of people generate actions based on perceptions they have of themselves. Expanding the perceptions of all people will raise them to new levels of action.

If people think only of themselves, raising the level of their behavior to a more idealistic plane would seem not only advantageous for the rest of us in society but evoke a sigh of relief from us all. There is little doubt in the minds of most of us that there is plenty of room for positive behavioral modification. Regarding the behavior level of more idealistic and farsighted people, the room for growth seems more limited. This perception, however, is false. There is no end to the degree of improvement anyone can make regarding their behavior. Only if people reach the all-encompassing totality of God, becoming God in total, can they no longer raise their behavior. But enough of this, for this is a discussion of relativistic limits, calculus, integration, and behavior.

It seems like an impossible task. It would have to be a percep-

tion all could understand, beautiful in its simplicity, inspiring in its potentiality, thought-provoking in its universality. The new perception would have to raise all people's level of thought and behavior towards not only others but towards themselves. Therefore, people must look to the motivation of the most idealistic to find what it would take to raise their spiritual glow, their commitment to the highest of ideals they are capable of perceiving. The highest level of idealism usually deals with the perception of the relationship between God and people. Presently, the most prevalent perception is a theistic concept: God is larger in size than our reality but separate from our reality. We are subservient to God. In essence, we are saying that God is limited in scope, for God and reality are two separate entities. God is not completely omnipresent, everywhere. In other words, God has size, a limit.

Theism generates a size to God. In order to expand people's perception of themselves and others, we are going to have to expand people's perception of God, the outer limit of thought. The perception of God, even of the most broad-minded idealist, orients around a God with size. We are going to have to change the concept of reality and people's function within reality, expand God and people's connection to God in order to include the deepest, most idealistic thinkers of humankind. Simply put, our God is too small. We will have to expand the concept of God. The only way is to establish a limitless model of God. This sounds complicated, but all we actually must do is blend the concepts of theism and pantheism, giving us panentheism.

As in theism, panentheism says God created reality and is bigger than reality. As in pantheism, panentheism says God traverses reality through awareness, one life form of which is human. Unique to itself, panentheism says people and God live in a symbiotic state, dependent upon each other; people have a significant purpose in connection to God, their souls are God, they are God. Significantly, panentheism also implies there are many realities within God other than human reality. That, in turn, implies there are many realities within God, which implies many life forms within God, which implies that although people cannot make do without God, God can make do without people.

With an acceptance of this expanded perception of people and their function within reality as well as an expanded perception that God has a need for people, we developed a means of expanding people's perception of themselves. With this concept in place, we have developed a means of initiating a behavioral change in all people, a change that would expand the compassion and respect all people, including the most idealistic, would feel and sense regarding themselves and others. How would this change society?

After refusing to redefine themselves in 1996, the violence and conflict generated by the battle over abortion and capital punishment still continues into 2050. Violence and conflict experienced over abortion and capital punishment refuses to resolve itself. It is a struggle over simple definition, a struggle perpetuated over the lack of agreement 50 years ago about what constitutes "life" and "death." Conflict and violence still runs rampant because people refuse to accept an elevated status for themselves. They still refuse to accept that they are more than just human, more than animal; they have significance in reality, a significance to God, they are a piece of God with a purpose for existence, and are needed by God to keep growing.

Without growth there are only two possibilities: permanent equilibrium, what we sometimes call permanent stagnation, or withering away into nonexistence. Maintaining a permanent state of equilibrium goes against everything we know, all laws of nature, all laws of logic. That leaves only one possibility for a God fitting the ideals of people and that is a growing God. That, in turn, opens the door for people to elevate their conception of themselves, their reality, and the very Creator of reality.

And what does this have to do with social ambiance? Everything. A person, seeing him/herself as a person, drives on the road, comes to a stop sign, stops, opens his door, throws out cigarette butts and garbage cluttering up the car, closes the door, and drives on. A person, seeing him/herself as a soul, as a piece of God, seeing others likewise, drives on the road, comes to a stop sign, stops, sees that others have littered or maybe that others haven't littered, consciously decides to respect the environment belonging to all, and keeps the garbage until coming to a trash barrel to dump the gar-

bage. Is this not a significant change in behavior? And this is on an almost laughable level. Consider how it would affect even more significant actions occurring in the 1990's.

People have reached a fork in the road – a time to pick out the decor of future society, a time to pick the theme which will permeate their social setting. The choices:

1. *Life is significant because it is life and as long as you live you have the potential to contribute to society; after the end of life, your life no longer has significance.*
2. *Life is significant because it is life and life has a significant purpose beyond reality; not even death can diminish life's contribution to eternity and you are a primary player.*

Choice One would lead to the perpetuation of our present system of social order. It would, in fact, allow the historical acceleration of the accumulation of power in the hands of a few to continue unchecked.

Choice Two, on the other hand, would elevate all people to an equal status of importance. It would change the concept of power to be used as a means of subjecting others to the concept of facilitating the human journey through reality. It would create a social environment that would be warm, comforting, reassuring, nonjudgmental, inspiring while at the same time perpetuating an aura of excitement and desire within people to move on to their next journey, the journey of spirituality. Choice Two would create a social ambiance that would generate a realization that the next journey, the journey after life, will be even better than this journey. Society would be filled with the anticipation that, in fact, the next journey most probably will be even more intense in its compassion and warmth than reality holds.

If society would choose to accept that people and God are tied closely together in a symbiotic manner, then not only do people have significance, but people are actually needed by God for a reason. People have a purpose! People are not only a tool of God, but a useful tool that actually adds to the very significance of God! Imagine God needing people! People are not just needed by God but are a portion of God. You and I are a piece of God. Your soul, my soul is a portion of God! Everyone has a purpose for journeying. One's journey is not over until it's over. Is productivity the purpose for existence? No! Traveling through life, experiencing life, is the purpose for life.

With choice two, the social ambiance is different. Now we do not see institutions to which moral people go in order to terminate their socially defined nonproductive lives. We see grand social centers to help the challenged with their life's journey, a place for all of us because we are all challenged in one way or another. We see a multitude of safe homes for women abused by their husbands who don't understand the significance of their spouse's journey in reality. We see police officers working as and in conjunction with social workers. We see schools mentoring and educating children viewed as the pillars of society's future. We see an environment sparkling and clean for all to enjoy as they journey. We see constant improvements within our parks, cities, countrysides, and institutions. We see, we feel, a society intent on leaving behind a total planet better than the one it started with. We see people reaching for the stars, aware that space itself is part of our environment and that all life forms have a purpose, a significance in reality.

Is God's survival dependent upon humans alone? No, God would not be foolish enough to put all Its eggs in one basket; but people now understand that God has put some eggs in our basket. We have significance. You and I have significance beyond today, beyond life.

The preceding documents flutter in the breeze as they are carried toward the morning sun shining on the streets of grey concrete. As the documents drift away, so too, does the hope of creating a social ambiance generated in the future by the perception that people's souls are a portion of God. Humans are not just creatures, servants of God, below God. You, I, all people, deserve respect for you and I are a portion of God. We have been given the free will to choose. It is our choice, your choice, my choice.

Just as surely as we vacillate in our decisions, the gentle winds of time move on and carry with them the fluttering sheets of paper upon which a new perception is set. People, due to vacillation, end up making a choice by not choosing. Leaders of humankind, unwilling to give up their power and control over others, have chosen to retain the status quo. People will remain people; people will remain who they have always been because their leaders choose not to change. The leaders of humankind have chosen to continue violence and conflict because they choose not to choose differently.

People, always seeking ways to empower themselves, are never given the opportunity to accept the most obvious – empowerment through a new perspective of themselves. People remain in subservience.

Slavery Is Slavery

Speculation 2100 A.D.: Humans are finding themselves to be less than they thought they were. People are being forced to face a new problem head on. They must choose to redefine God or keep the old definition, for they have found their Creator.

Cytologists and geneticists trace the bio-molecular structure of the mitochondria of the human cell back to what they believe to be the origin of humans. The first woman, "Eve," is now believed not only to be a possibility by scientists, but she could also be a genetically manipulated hybrid of an early form of earth mammal combined with a genetically unknown life form alien to earth. The genetic manipulation appears to have taken place approximately ten thousand to fifteen thousand years ago. Anthropologists are now studying the evidence and have no theory regarding why any extraterrestrials would combine its genes with an early form of earth mammal. Some experts, however, believe that humans may be a genetic manipulation of earthly life intended to generate semi-intelligent life forms to act as earthbound labor for a more intelligent species alien to earth. Theoretically, this would have been an excellent means of developing and pacifying the primitive and hostile environmental potential of the earth.

To put it more bluntly, humans may have been developed as an environmentally compatible slave to tame planet earth. Humankind: a biologically created work force intended to convert earth into an industrially efficient planetary factory and recreation center for some as yet unknown alien life form? Is earth a living, thriving planet intended to be turned over to another life form after it has been groomed and prepared for the initial full scale deployment of this new population? Imagine earth as a fully developed planet with a work force knowledgeable and trained in all the intricacies of environmental, social, industrial, technological, and biological webs established upon it, maintained by the very self-supporting, self-educating, self-reproducing slave labor force created by the owners of the primitive planet earth. If this is the case, our creators indubitably would be coming back at some future date to claim their newly transformed planetary body. Our creators could just be waiting for the most opportune time to return and settle into their new home.

The question becomes, what will they find when they get here? Will they find what they hope for? Will they find a planet thriving, a planet teeming with a slave labor force psychologically ripe for subjugation because they are divided and confused over their purpose in reality? This division and confusion would be generated by constant violence and conflict due to the lack of a universally accepted, broad, unifying philosophy. This philosophy would establish, without a doubt, the concept that all people operate on an equal status with one another and prepare them to accept themselves as equals with any and all life forms encountered within this universe.

Humankind lacks a universal philosophy, a rationality that would lead them to the understanding that they have equal significance relative to other extraterrestrial life forms, which they may be forced to face at some future date. Humans lack a universal philosophy broad enough or strong enough to elevate them to a level so high that even meeting God face to face would not cause them to doubt their significance in reality. People lack the perspective of their purpose that would raise their significance out of the realm of this reality and into a perspective of major significance for the realm of eternity itself, a time that follows "life" itself, reality itself.

This basic void humankind has regarding a lofty significance for themselves in reality will surely be the fundamental reason our creators may find a planet brimming over with a maintenance work force ready and thirsting for a master to solve their social problems of violence and conflict and provide the leadership necessary to bring peace and tranquillity. Humanity is ready to accept subjugation to a superior life form in exchange for new medical knowledge and raising the status of all people to a level of comfort and security. This exchange would be at no cost for people other than a willingness to serve their Creator, which many will profess we have been doing anyway, for is our Creator not God?

Theism has long professed that people are humble servants of their Creator, indoctrinated over the last ten thousand years to be a loyal servant to God. How can we go against our traditions generated over the last ten thousand years? How can we now, after having been loyal subjects through faith, suddenly turn away from our God, our Creator? How can we, after having accepted ten thousand years of indoctrination regarding our purpose for being created, suddenly change our minds, refuse to be a loyal servant, and begin to say we have a higher purpose than to serve God? Half the world's population immediately falls in line with its Creator and accepts its long professed religion of servitude and now understands just who "God" is. A sigh of relief is heard around the world as the massive religious and minuscule philosophical segments, for the most part, accept the inevitable: we have come face to face with our God.

The other half of the world is skeptical and wonders as to our true calling. Slavery is slavery. If we were consciously developed as a labor force intended to tame a wild, primitive world, does that mean we cannot rise above such a status level of servitude? Could not our purpose for existence have been one thing, but then risen to a new height in an unpredictable manner out of the control of our creator? Is our creator really God or is God greater than that; is God not really the creator of reality itself? Must we resign ourselves to the level for which we were initially intended? Don't we have the right to rise above our initially intended function and follow our own journey? Don't we have a soul?

Religion and philosophy find themselves in the middle of a major battle, a battle of perception. If we are just a tool developed to tame the planet earth, doesn't this mean we should maintain our loyalty and continue in the service of "God?" Wouldn't this mean our God is, in actuality, another life form traversing this reality in a more advanced state than us and, as such, shouldn't we accept our place in reality as being just what we were created to be?

Our present perception of ourselves as servants of God would force us into a bitterly divisive debate unsolvable in a globally unifying manner. Some would believe that our purpose in reality is to glorify our Creator, and on the other side, others would believe we have a purpose and significance in reality beyond that of glorifying our Creator. Ten percent of us on one side and ten percent of us on the other side of the battlefield. The other eighty percent would be caught in the middle, finding themselves lost between the two warring factions. It would be a battle between the idealists with heads held high working hand in hand with God to expand God's significance beyond reality vs. the conventionalists with heads bowed before their God, working to remain servants of God, striving to keep a God of limited size. Is this debate even solvable?

On the one hand, with our present perception of inferiority to God, the answer would be, No, the problem is not solvable. And so it is that through our perception of ourselves and God, we remain servants of God. We are slaves of God. Or are we slaves of another intelligent life form we call God? What's the difference? Slavery is slavery. Subjugation is subjugation.

On the other hand, with the perception of panentheism that we are not just human, but are the soul, that our soul is God traveling realities, the answer would be, Yes, the problem is solvable. With this perception, we would understand that we were created by God in order to expand Its very omniscience, omnipotence, and omnipresence. We would understand that we may have been created by a more intelligent life form for the particular purpose of taming and maintaining a planetary body, but we would also understand that whether by accident or intentionally, once we were given awareness and the ability to rationalize, we were given a soul. We are no longer just a body; our essence is our soul. Our body and mind are mechanisms by which our awareness, our rationality, our essence, our soul, God, travels reality. We travel to learn and experience, to grow. As such, our body and mind have no right to subjugate ourselves or others and have no right to relegate souls to a position of servitude. This leads to the basic principle that no one, not even other intelligent life forms, has the right to subjugate others.

Taking this position after the fact, however, is a little late for damage control, for much of the damage will already have been done. Much of humanity will, through faith in what religious institutions have professed over the last ten thousand years, accept their position of servitude, of subjugation, of glorification to God. For us, at this point, to accept that we are now all of a sudden God, will be too late and we will have put ourselves in a position of eternal servitude with no eternity to go to. If this, in fact, turned out to be the scenario, we would no doubt be in a very precarious position.

But we are phenomenally resilient animals. The idealists would no doubt cling to their ideals with zest and fanaticism while the sheep fall in line with the masters.

The pacification of earth and humankind would not take place peacefully. Humankind has never been a species easily subjugated. A battle of major proportions would undoubtedly result. The idealist would have the enthusiasm, motivation, and vision. The subjugated and resigned would have the numbers and social organization, as has always been the case throughout history.

Now, however, the resigned would also have their new masters as allies. Battles in our past have often centered around attempts at raising humankind to a higher level of significance. These battles have never been easy and have always been bloody. This battle will be no different. In fact, this battle will be our most difficult because it will be a battle to maintain our uniqueness and independence, not upon earth and within our own species, but rather in terms of the very outer limits of the universe. It would be a battle to establish our significance within reality. We would, once again, be in a battle over the humiliating degrading concept of slavery.

All of this could have been prevented if we had simply accepted a symbiotic relationship with God a long time ago. If we had accepted our soul as our essence and then developed the logic for its existence in the first place, this understanding, this acceptance of panentheism, would have caused us to raise our perception of ourselves to that of God traveling.

Panentheism would have been a concept that no discovery could have shaken. It would have united all people to support a "cause" of universal tolerance. It would have placed humankind as a species into the camp of all intelligent beings within the universe – a band of allies bonded by their support of the right of all souls to travel uninhibited and their subsequent demand for the respect of any traveling life form to remain unique and free of subjugation and abuse. With panentheism, people would belong to a camp of allies that would always have the idealism and vision of optimism on their side. This is a camp idealists intuitively know must exist or at least should exist out there in the heavens. This is a camp filled with allies standing tall and proud of their principles, filled with warmth, compassion, loyalty, comradeship, and vision.

With panentheism, we could step into the heavens knowing we had allies before we even knew who they were or even if they actually existed. We would step into the heavens knowing that if opposing camps did exist somewhere in the stars, that we had already committed ourselves to a camp of vision and high ideals. We would step into the heavens proud and tall. We would find a common cause shared by other beings – allies awaiting our arrival into space, bound by the common belief that slavery is slavery and no person, no soul, has the right to interfere with the journey of another. No one has the right to enslave another soul.

And if this camp doesn't exist? Then what a glorious position for humankind, for we would be the first members of just such an idealistic, tolerant, respecting, principled, rightfully proud camp. We would be the leaders for a higher level of idealism.

Humanity Sentenced To Life

Speculation 2150 A.D.: Humans ride the tides of time like surfers in a storm. This year brings with it new insights; people are violent because they have violence in their genes. Within fifty years, the theory generated by cytologists and geneticists that humankind is a hybrid of earth genes and extraterrestrial genes starts to crumble. As much as humankind wishes to breath a sigh of relief, it cannot for anthropologists and archeologists have uncovered some fascinating finds.

Atlantis has been found and, with it, some ill-preserved records and specimens of her occupants. Over the next ten years, through technological ingenuity and DNA analysis, the true story of our origin begins to unfold.

Humans, it appears, are not in any way native to earth. The archeological findings indicate that we were brought to earth fifteen thousand years ago. Computer analysis, although incomplete and based upon revolutionary new but untested computer models, shows with a large degree of certainty that the cytology theory had some validity but was incorrect in its perception of people as a genetic hybrid of alien and earth life forms. In fact, we appear to be alien to earth, originating totally outside the earth's environs.

Partially preserved art work and records found in Atlantis indicate that several small colonies were established at the same time but at various locations upon earth. The records do not indicate exactly how many colonies were established, but they do seem to imply the original group was split into five subgroups. Atlantis appears to have sprung up from one of these five subgroups. The original space travelers appear to have been delivered to earth as an alternative means of isolating them from their original society outside of earth. They were brought here by a society that opposed the concept of permanent confinement of its members within its own society. Small groups of extraterrestrials were sentenced to live out their lives on earth as a means of banishing them from their own societies. Ostracism – the most extreme action of a species seeking to protect itself from small numbers of its society.

Initial study reveals the startling fact that the ostracized individuals were violent incorrigibles. We find the originality of a continental penal colony is not originality personified. Australia is nothing other than an unconscious reversion to our past rational thought process of finding a means of self-protection while respecting the concept of life. If it isn't historians, scientists, philosophers, sociologists, mathematicians, prophets, and mystics, it's religious institutions confronting us with our inferiority. Why can't we just raise perceptions of ourselves to the highest level attainable and forego all the bitter conflicts and introspection new discoveries keep shoving into our face? Will we find no rest, no peace from our constant exposure to subjugating and degrading discoveries? How ironic that we become physically weary and mentally fatigued from violence and conflict, the very actions that now appear to have caused us to be isolated from our own society in the first place.

Why do we refuse to raise ourselves to the level of God Itself and accept the logic that we have a purpose in reality, we are significant regardless of any discoveries our natural persistent characteristic of curiosity may reveal as we advance ourselves and society? Why not accept the philosophy of panentheism and establish the simple concept that the essence of our being is the spirit, that our essence is the soul? After all, a perception of this magnitude would allow us to shuck away our husk, the body and mind, as nothing other than tools of the soul.

Panentheism is a universal philosophy, a process of elevating our essence to the level of God. The soul is an essence isolated from God and located within us for a purpose. Humans and God exist in a loving symbiotic relationship. God is greater in scope than us, but is us nonetheless. We are, in essence, a soul, a piece of God and therefore God Itself. We are, therefore, equal to God. We have a significant role to play in God's personal development.

Panentheism is a perception of existence. Panentheism does not replace any cultures, traditions or religions; it is a means of finding purpose for a species, for individuals. It is a new foundation for our present crumbling, shortsighted, self-degrading foundations. Our present foundations commit us to an eternity of servitude, a state of being that establishes the social concept of servitude and worth of one person over another within every social structure we create. One person is valued over another; one person's worth is judged to be greater than another. We find it impossible to eradicate this concept, for it permeates the very relation between ourselves and God.

And yet we have an option; we can eliminate this stigmatizing, degrading, shallow-minded philosophy of theism. We have the choice; we could choose to elevate our purpose within reality to a new level that would rationalize a positive significance for ourselves in reality, capable of withstanding any startling unexpected turn of events regarding anything we discover, conceive or confront. The only exception would be us finding actual proof that we were truly supposed to be insignificant. This is a proof, however, which would never be accepted by us regardless of its validity, for we are ingenious and original enough to find a means of rationalizing our way out of even a paradox of that nature.

But now we find we are unable to release ourselves of fifteen thousand years of traditional servitude and inferiority. We remain subservient and subjugated because of a philosophy generated as an intentional action directed towards keeping our shame hidden away in a closet. We find that not only do individuals within our ranks keep skeletons hidden in the closet, but that our entirety as a species is oriented around the false premise that we were created by God. This concept comes crumbling down like an antiquated skyscraper subjected to the expertise of an explosive expert. We open our closet only to find a hidden skeleton, none other than what we have been seeking throughout existence. We seek to uncover the mystery of our origination. We seek our biological origin and are confronted with the most frightening of all nightmares: we are criminals, rejects of a society. We are an unwanted element. Our origin has been sealed away in a closet by our own biological parents acting out of shame and out of fear that future generations may not be able to rise above their historical roots of violence.

Our original ancestors were not ignorant. They understood that there is no better way to contain a genetic trait of violence than to lock that knowledge away in the closet and then propagate the philosophical perception that we are inferior to God, that we are inferior to our Creator, a Creator that professes love and peace. A philosophy of this nature would humble us and might contain our propensity toward violence long enough for our future offspring to establish a more advanced philosophy, believable and understood by all, capable of logically raising incorrigibles above the self-serving actions of violence directed towards others and directed towards even one's self.

A universally contrived plan could have been conjured up when the original settlers were on board a craft bringing them to their penal colony. Imagine it, incorrigibles, through the long nights of space travel, find a common cause, a higher vision and establish common ground for actions to begin the development of a new planet. A journey through space originating in crime results in a plan immersed in hope, vision, and resolve to establish a new beginning for the future generations to come. Criminals create a vision wrapped in the idealism that all events have the potential for "good." A vision, an inspiration, is hatched in the confines of space, evolving through forced isolation, and germinating on a hostile, out-of-the-way planet. The vision is that the generation to be, born from the loins of incorrigibles, may someday stand tall and proud as they enter the magnificence of space to take on a position of leadership and strength regarding the significance of the individual over the species. A new member of the Milky Way originating as incorrigibles may be ready to join others in their crusade to do away with subjugation and dominance so that all souls may journey in peace and harmony.

Ah, but sadly, we are not ready for such an exciting, inspiring existence. Our perception of ourselves as servants inferior to our Creator has taken on too strong a hold and we reject our potential as an equal to God. We are not ready to take on responsibility of this magnitude. We are too unsure of ourselves. We cannot shake the fear of eternal hell we may face for wanting to reevaluate our place in reality. We cannot shake the fear, handed down throughout all of our earthly existence, that if we release our subjugation to our Creator, we will bring on a punishment of eternal fire and damnation through seeking the truth, to eliminate violence, and to eliminate our fears.

We originate from a violent past and, as such, are unable to shake off our natural inheritance. We are nothing other than a race, a species, of rejects. We are offspring of violent incorrigibles. We might as well resign ourselves to a future of violence and move on to the future, carrying violence with us, for we have discovered our past before we were ready. In a juvenile state, we are unwilling to accept our responsibility within reality and look at our true source of origin. We become resigned to our genetic past of violence.

How sad for us, how sad for future generations to come, how sad for those with whom we shall come in contact, for we have evolved more technologically than philosophically, and this has made all the difference. We are not yet ready to accept our significance in eternity. We cling to our status of servitude, conflict, and violence. We carry these very traits into the heavens and earth now becomes the exporter of what forced our banishment to a primitive planet in the first place. Earth is now in a position of exporting concepts of individual worth of one over another, status levels, manipulation of others for the "greater good," violence, subjugation, and conflict.

We are falling into the very depths of corruption our original forefathers had planned so diligently to avoid. Our forefathers hid skeletons in the closet in the hopes that future generations would not fall into the same behavior patterns they had taken. We open the closet in the hopes of finding our true purpose in reality and find what we fear most. We find ourselves. We are unable to rationalize a philosophy strong enough to raise us above who we were in the past. Due to a small-minded philosophy, we find truth in the statement, "Like father, like son."

Trapped

Speculation 2200 A.D.: A new dilemma arises and we finally understand we are nothing but a bug in a bottle. We fall into despair and depression for we can find no way out. We find the limit, the walls containing our universe, and realize our own significance is limited.

Mathematics is the cutting edge of science, the universal language used to describe and define our universe. It is a learned way of thinking that has finally earned the respect it has so long deserved. Mathematics turns out to be universal to all life forms throughout the reality we travel.

Topology is a field of mathematics that started by defining a plane, a piece of paper, with only one side. One can paint the inside and outside surface of a ring of paper made by gluing two ends of a strip of paper together. Once painting the inside of the ring red, one can then paint the outside of the ring green. If, however, one puts a single twist in the paper before gluing the ends together, one obtains what is known in topology as a Mobius strip. The ring has only one side and can only be painted one color, since if one puts a paint brush on any point and paints the total surface, one will, without picking up the paper and turning it over, end up with all surfaces painted red because the ring now only has one side. Thus, a two sided ring becomes a one sided ring. This leads to a startling concept regarding humanity, the universe, and eternity.

Topological mathematics developed the Klein bottle in the 1900's, a three dimensional bottle in three dimensional space that only has two dimensions. What does this mean? Everyone was saying, "So, what?" All but a few theoretical mathematicians let the concept go. Now, however, two hundred years later, the Klein bottle resurfaces. Scientists have found what appears to be the outer limits of our universe. Mathematicians have plotted its configuration to be an exact replica of the inside of a Klein bottle. Most bottles are three dimensional and have an inside and outside. The Klein bottle, however, is a three dimensional bottle having only two dimensions.

A Klein bottle appears to those on the outside as having no inside. On the other hand, to those inside, the Klein bottle appears to have no outside.

The universe surrounded by God is like a bottle that, to someone outside the bottle, appears to have no inside and to someone on the inside, it appears to have no outside. To God, the bottle appears to have no inside. God, however, having created the Klein bottle and having been in and out of these bottles many times, knows differently. God knows exactly why It created the bottle and also knows the emptiness It feels. The empty feeling God senses is the same empty feeling we feel when we lose a loved one, when we lose a limb. God senses a loss because It *is* missing a portion of Itself. It is missing the portions of Itself It has sent into seemingly infinite numbers of Klein bottles, the many Klein bottles It has created within Itself and dispersed throughout Itself. A sense of loss, a sense of attachment, a sense of connection, a sense of love, a sense of anticipation for the inevitable reunion to follow and on and on it goes for God has no limit, not even a limit to Its potential for growth. The very reason God created these Klein bottles was the need for growth.

To those on the inside, there are two choices. In both cases, the concept of the Klein bottle begins much the same but ends differently, as we shall see.

Science in 2200 has found there is a boundary to our universe. Science, having found the boundary, now knows that the universe through which we travel has an outside. Our universe has a limit. We, defined by the boundary of the universe, have found our limit. We are indeed insignificant. With no significance comes the destruction of hope. The world is about to be thrown into a bottomless pit of depression, despair, and acceptance of its insignificance.

We swirl about in our continual eddy of unresolved perception of our significance in reality. This is an eddy whose energy source is not understanding what reality and the purpose of reality are. We constantly, within our subconscious, directly tie our size of significance to the size of reality. We have wedded the concept of infinity to our reality because we desperately want our significance to be infinitely important. Now we have found reality to be finite and, in turn, found ourselves to be finite in significance. With this understanding, we realize we are insignificant relative to the infinite vastness that must extend beyond the boundaries of our reality – a vastness we will most likely never see.

We have always clung to the hope that our universe was infinite, for an infinite universe meant we had the possibility for infinite significance. Now, we find we are confined within a bounded, limited Klein bottle and the universe must also be bounded, limited in significance. Science sees no possibility of cracking through the wall of the Klein universe. Theoretically, a Klein bottle, a Klein universe, has, for someone on the outside, no way of being entered and for someone on the inside, a Klein universe has no way of being exited. We are confined in a bottle like a bug in a jar.

With the realization of the universe having a boundary, a limit, we sense our true insignificance to God and desperately grasp the historically battered concept that we are a servant of God and, as such, must spread God's message throughout the universe. We accept that we are meant to act as a messenger of God and are meant to bring all life forms throughout the universe to their knees in praise of God the Almighty. All resources, all energy, must be poured into today in order to speed up the process of proselytizing, spreading the word, for unbelievers will surely suffer the consequence of hell and we will be responsible and as such, will also suffer.

The environment begins to feel the onslaught of the desperation of our intensity as it succumbs to the needs of our ambition to spread the knowledge of God's purpose for life, God's desire to be glorified. With the discovery of a boundary to our universe, we finally understand our purpose. And as our nature dictates, reinforced with an indisputable understanding of purpose, we begin to change gears, moving our economy into a war mode.

Space weapons and space fleets are begun in earnest. Space colonies spring up on the moon as rapidly as the architectural plans can be drawn. Mining of Mars and asteroids moves into full swing as the huge new mega-factories on earth pump out space materials. Brazil becomes the new found land of hope as its tropical forests give way to mineral extracting methods that are the pride of humanity. Oceans become farms and ranches, feeding a human population approaching a hundred billion for the first time in our history. Land becomes a scarce resource for mega-factories, megalopolises, and recreational areas overburdened with the needs of the swarm of humanity striving to spread its influence into the near heavens.

Our brief dance with despair over our insignificance in reality has been replaced with understanding our purpose in reality, our subservience to God. We come to terms with our servitude as an instrument of God intended to glorify God. We spread the word into the far reaches of space, and begin an onslaught of the very earth God provided us as the stepping stone into the unknown.

We begin earnestly ravaging the earth with our intentions of spreading a message induced by the very image of our limited purpose in reality. Not understanding that our significance lies beyond this reality and not within this limited universe, we begin an onslaught of earth and her surroundings the likes of which history has never seen.

We are faced with two choices: to be subservient or to be a piece of God. Two distinctly different concepts generate two distinctly different paths for us as we find the limit to our universe. The fork in the road is not the discovery of the boundary of our universe, our reality. The fork in the road is how we choose to handle ourselves if we find our universe has a limit, if we find that we are confined in a bottle. How we handle ourselves, in turn, is determined by how we perceive ourselves, what we perceive our significance is in terms of our relationship to God and eternity.

Our present choice is theism, a philosophical perception of subservience, a choice generating actions of desperation to act as a servant of God, a tool of God having the specific purpose of spreading "the word," glorifying God by using the earth, using people, using all to expand our concepts of unlimited insignificance. We are a tool of God, traversing reality to expand the universal choir whose function is to spend our days singing God's praises and then to die, no longer significant. This subservience is reinforced by the understanding that our universe has size, which interprets into our having relative insignificance. How shortsighted, egocentric, and sensually hedonistic we are.

The other choice is panentheism, a philosophical perception of equality to God, generating patience, tender handling, hope for the earth, for us, and for everything with which we come into contact. Equality to God is a perception that generates respect for all life forms we encounter and environments we step into. Equality is reinforced with the understanding that our universe has size which interprets into our magnificent significance. We are a tool of God, traversing reality to expand Its very self. We, God, travel reality to expand upon our own infinity and then die, becoming even more significant through reinfusion back into God. As we are reinfused back into God, we carry a new awareness, an awareness we have acquired through our journey within the Klein bottle universe, an awareness that will allow God to actually grow and, through growth, become an even greater God. Equality to God, panentheism, leads to a perception that builds the magnificence of God. Panentheism leads to an understanding of how we are to build and expand within our reality, using the perception of God, the image of God as our Guide, for we are God.

We can build a new future by submersion in the perception of dark subservience or acceptance of the concept of the glorious light of equality to God. We have free will to choose and can choose to defy the laws of reality and cling to the desire to maintain our historic perceptions of God, thus choosing subservience out of fear of change. Or we can bond with nature and the laws of our reality and can choose to raise our status to the level of God – a choice based on logic, immersed in hope. It is your choice, my choice.

If we remain submerged in the cold dark waters of subservience, our significance will shrivel up and shrink into insignificance. On the other hand, if we rise above the cold waters of subservience into the warmth of the light of equality, our significance will expand and grow.

Two choices: one of subservience and one of magnificence. There appears to be no question as to which choice holds the greatest potential, but we are a stubborn creature and thus still cannot commit ourselves. We choose by not choosing, and so the violence and conflict continue into the future as we use our free will by not using free will.

We move to the quarter millennium and find ourselves trapped in a bottle because we refuse to acknowledge that our awareness, our soul, has significance beyond the material world, beyond the bottle. We are a materialistic creature, indeed.

Collapse

Speculation 2250 A.D.: If we thought we were going to get out of the bottle before it collapsed, we were sadly mistaken. 2250 proves to be a very sobering year. We soon discover that our prison, the Klein bottle, is not eternal. We are about to discover there is a big difference between emptiness and nothingness. We are about to realize that our universe collapsing into nothingness may appear to be a threatening concept, but it may be far less traumatic than collapsing into emptiness.

Science and technology continue to inspire and amaze us. In fifty short years, we have developed technology capable of adjusting for the Klein bottle effect that had previously distorted our ability to find the boundary of the universe. The boundary is now fully mapped and we are beginning to dream of voyages to the far reaches of the galaxy and even beyond. There appears to be no end to the borders of our influence, other than the far distant boundary of the universe itself.

The boundary of the universe is smooth as glass yet made of no apparent physical substance. It appears to be impenetrable by anything of which we are aware. The boundary is an apparent force field of some type that we cannot begin to comprehend, for it appears to defy all laws of physics. It turns away all energy or matter emissions we generate and project in its direction. The energy emissions we direct at it become redirected into the bottle in a perfectly predictable manner defined by the mathematics describing behavior of matter and energy contained within a Klein bottle topology. The Klein bottle appears to be an impenetrable container bounding reality itself. It appears that we have no means at our disposal, no source of energy available to us, that will ever be able to defy the boundaries of reality. We are living in a bottle like a butterfly in a glass jar.

As if this weren't insulting enough to our ego, science has, in addition, found massive unexpected reserves of matter, previously laying unseen behind the region of our Klein bottle that folds back upon itself. There is now no doubt that there is more than enough matter in space to cause the reverse of the big bang. The universe is going to implode in the far future and we will be snuffed out in the process.

The boundary of the Klein bottle has been fully mapped and found to be almost perfectly smooth on all of its surfaces, including the section that folds back upon itself. There is only one exception to the smoothness of the mappings and that appears on only a small sector of the internal boundary of the Klein configuration. At this point, science has no explanation regarding what this anomaly is, but one thing is certain, it has no connection either to the fact that we exist in a bottle, a Klein bottle, nor does it have any relationship to the amount of mass in the universe. The big bang will reverse itself and take us with it.

Science has confirmed the perfection of God through the mapping of the Klein configuration of the universe, our own reality. The only insignificant hitch is the minute glitch found on one sector of the boundary of space. Science, with investigation, will overcome the mystery of the minute glitch for nothing has stood unsolvable before us and our God. With more investigation, science finds the minute location on the boundary of our universe is emitting a phenomenal quantity of energy. This is a strange phenomenon but has little significance at this most traumatic time – a time when we first realize that reality will not go on forever.

All matter, the universe, humans themselves, are apparently nothing but a flicker in eternity – a temporary malformation of energy. We are not only contained in a bottle but a bottle that, compared to eternity, has a relatively short life span. How depressing to realize that we and our universe may eventually collapse into nothingness, something which has absolutely no apparent connection to us, the servants of God. How will religion and philosophy manage to spiritually and philosophically deal with this new obstacle?

Religious institutions continuing to embrace a traditional philosophy will have to come to terms with each other in order to come to terms with our new discoveries. The western approach emanating from the external study of people and God and the eastern approach emanating from the internal study of people and God must now blend into a hybrid format of both an external and internal glorification of God, of serving God. Humans, the loyal servants, now exist as a total unit. Traditional and classical religious institutions profess that we have no significance but to sing praises and expand the number of subservients God has. What greater significance could be possible than to serve the Almighty directly, to establish a heavenly choir resonating from one end of the universe to the other?

Even more resolved to increase our significance to God, we disregard the pollution and human trauma we generate in order to expand God's presence in reality. The greater we make God, the greater Its servants are, and that means an increase in significance for us. We are unconcerned with pollution we lay in the paths of people to come, for our journey has a time limit. We are willing to continue to abuse not only our environment but everyone around us in order to serve God, raise God to the highest heights. We begin abusing ourselves as we submit to the whims of others as they march to the holy crusades in space, as they move to glorify God.

How unfortunate for the living, how unfortunate for the souls to come. We could have taken another tact. We could have accepted another perception of ourselves. We could have accepted that our significance lies in a greater reality than our own. We could have accepted that reality lies within God and we are but a machine carrying God. The panentheistic concept is simple. We travel reality within a Klein bottle for a purpose. We travel innocently disconnected from our source, from God. We travel spiritually disconnected from God in order to learn, create, and experience.

This approach is no great savior. This philosophy, panentheism, does, however, through its uniqueness, offer a new outlook regarding the possibility of the implosion of the universe. Panentheism, rather than generating a cloud of depression and resignation, would generate the strengthened resolution to learn as much as we could in the time we have, for that, as described by panentheism, is our purpose in reality.

Reality has a time frame for existence, which means we have a time frame to accomplish as much as we can and we all know we work more efficiently, responsively, determinedly when we are confronted by a deadline, especially a deadline to existence.

Panentheism would provide us with an understanding that the end of our reality does not diminish what we have learned, created, and experienced. What we have learned, created, and experienced will be carried to what lies beyond our little Klein bottle, our small reality, and the collapse of our universe will not destroy what has been carried outside of it. What has been taken to God will not be destroyed by the collapse of our reality.

But we ask, "What if God transcends reality? What if our reality, our Klein universe, is not immersed within God?" The answer is simple with our present, traditional theistic approach; we and our universe would disappear into emptiness. Our reality would disappear into a void and there would be no place to go; the soul would have to wander forever in the darkness of a void. This would be much worse than what panentheism has to offer. Under panentheism, reality immersed within God, we would understand that our reality imploding would mean disappearing into nothingness with God surrounding reality. This nothingness would force us to disappear into the arms of God as our reality dissolves. It means your soul has a place to go. You, your soul, will be surrounded by God, a light in the midst of uncertainty.

Again, we are confronted by a fork in the road of our journey. We have a choice, once again, to remain subservient to God, to remain at a lower status below God, eventually only to collapse into emptiness; or we can choose to raise our perception of ourselves to a new level equal to God, literally a portion of God traveling reality. We would again collapse, but this time into nothingness, leaving our naked souls enveloped in the arms of God.

We approach the middle of the millennium tied to conflict and violence, unable to define ourselves well enough to avoid trauma generated by new knowledge, the most powerful of all forces in the heavens. We can choose the darkness of emptiness or the light, warmth, and serenity of material nothingness. What a choice and still we waver as we move on through time.

The Nightmare

Speculation 2300 A.D.: We find one can dream in a dream. Reality is a figment of one's imagination, caught up in the nightmare of the dream of time.

Does time exist? Mathematicians and physicists have long held that we exist within a reality of four dimensions, three dimensions defining space and the fourth dimension defined by time. Within our reality as we define it, things only exist in reality at a certain point in time. We live within a reality defined by time. And what if time is not real but is instead a perception created by a creator dreaming? Then we are but a dream created by one's self. Then everything is a figment of one's imagination. In such a scenario, time would become finite rather than infinite. Time would cease to exist once one awakened.

And what then would reality be? It would be what lies beyond our dream, or should I say what lies beyond your dream for "we" would no longer exist. Would this make reality any less significant? This is no different a scenario than the one we hold onto presently within the dream. We visualize ourselves traversing a reality, a dream, created in the mind of God. You say, "No, no we are real!"

But would this make reality any less real, any less significant? It would if you are a part of God's dream and perceive yourself to be a servant of God. For then you become a part of a dream existing for but a time and, within this time frame, you perpetuate a world of violence and pain. Sadly, you are also continuing to perpetuate such a world. Even more tragic, you become a carrier spreading the concepts throughout the far reaches of God's dream, expanding it throughout time itself.

If, on the other hand, it turns out that everything around us, around you, is a dream, a figment of your imagination, do you want to awaken from a nightmare within which you had subjected yourself to eternal servitude, submission, and pain? Do you want to awaken to the awareness that you were responsible for generating just such a concept? You would awaken in a void, in dark isolation, with a new awareness of being inflicted with pain, of being subjugated, of being traumatized by beings you create. That is what you would be generating in your dreams – a state, the concept, of being a servant of a God that is nowhere to be seen. You would be creating within your dream a reality that generates status, superiority, abusive power, and sensual hedonism.

If all is but a figment of your imagination, a dream you are having, control it. Do not awaken to total isolation and darkness thinking there may be another like yourself somewhere out there waiting to subjugate and dominate you. The dream state you are generating, have generated, is by no means useless for it will heighten your awareness of just such a possible encounter. If such is the case, you will awaken to the fact that the possibility exists as you have already taught yourself within your dream. The dream of conflict and violence may have been truly a nightmare, but it will have been of value nonetheless. There is no doubt that becoming aware of just such a possibility has its benefits. It is unquestionably beneficial to generate the awareness of the possibility of an interaction aimed at subjugation and dominance intended to benefit the intruder at your expense. You would want the knowledge of the possibility of just such an occurrence for, with awareness, comes the ability to prepare to subvert such an event.

Certainly you want to be ready for just such an encounter as you awaken into a void of blackness; however, why not also be ready to offer an alternative to such an encounter, to an intruder that may enter your non-dreaming space of darkness and isolation? You could be ready to offer an alternative philosophy to your first contact in the void outside yourself. You could be ready to offer a unique concept, a unique philosophy, that would portray the advantages of a journey where you travel together in a state of mutual respect for each other's unique capabilities and insights. You would offer a journey built upon a bond of trust and total acceptance, a bond recognizing that both you and your new companion may be entities within a God that needs you both.

You could offer your potentially new, potentially first companion, a concept of God waiting for the two of you to work together to glean knowledge and create in order to bring along newness for It. With an increase in the omniscience of your God would come the increase in your Creator's omnipresence. An increase in knowledge would, by definition, be an increase in awareness which, in turn, is an increase of at least one form of presence. With knowledge comes power, and so it is that your Creator would automatically increase in power as it increased in knowledge with the aid of your dreams, dreams you experience as you lay alone in a realm of darkness, fearful yet hopeful of encountering a companion with whom to share your travels. You hope to awaken to a companion who would take away the terror of the blackness, the all-consuming void within which you exist – alone.

You wait with your perpetual optimistic thoughts that you shall someday be joined. You know you must have a Creator of your own. How could it be otherwise, for you have been able to perceive of just such an entity, which in turn leads you to believe that just such an entity exists. You wait in a void of emptiness, knowing you must have some significance or why would you exist in the first place? You wait in darkness as you drift off to dream of a beautiful blue and white earth circling a wondrous yellow star set against a background of black velvet studded with infinite numbers of emeralds, diamonds, rubies, sapphires, onyx, aquamarines, pearls ablaze with color and warmth. You constantly return to this dream which, when more closely inspected, is found to have several locations riddled with violence and conflict, hate and rejection, jealousy and desire to dominate, abuse of power and infliction of pain, inferiority and superiority perception – all rendered possible due to a minor misconception within your dream. Entities within the dream do not understand they are entities of your dream, but rather believe they are entities unto themselves and as such, they believe falsely that they exist independent of you, the creator of the dream. These entities call themselves "people."

How ludicrous, how laughable, what a sham, for how could they perceive themselves to be independent of you? You are their creator! How could they possibly think you would create them, conjure them up, for no reason at all? How do they possibly think they could exist independent of you and enter an existence of "hell" apart from you when there is nothing outside of you of which even you are aware? These isolated fragments of existence worry you for they could conceivably spread their thought patterns of violence and conflict. They could infect your dream with the disease of subjugation and despair. They are proving to be your worst nightmare. Your only hope is for them to expand their perceptions of themselves and to realize the illogic of their logic before they spread their propensity for violence and conflict. Ironically, they spread their disease of inflicting pain and trauma through their adamant desire to remain subservient to you rather than take on independence, the responsibility of free will to choose as they travel the dream you created. They travel in a fog of righteousness with a false loyalty that could infect your entire dream.

You are compelled to feel a certain sense of admiration for them, their resolve, and their ingenuity as they scurry about attempting to maintain their state of awe and loyalty to you. But there also is no doubt that they could cause a great deal of pain for you. They could turn into a true night terror. You have no desire to awaken once again into the blackness surrounding you, screaming aloud into the void where there is no one to hear. You do not wish to awaken afraid to fall asleep and begin dreaming again of a beautiful, vast, warm, compassionate existence giving way to the nightmare of violence and pain. You do not wish to begin an endless cycle of awakening to your silent screams being projected into a vacuum of loneliness.

If only these entities within your dreams would stop their violence, stop the endlessly expanding spiral of their infliction of pain and open their minds to the wondrous possibilities that await them. If only they would realize they have free will, they have a purpose, they have significance even if they are only in a dream. If only they would realize the pain they are generating and would decide to end their persistent cycle of violence through a small change in perception, the realization that they are you. If only they would accept that their reality, they themselves, are a part of you, teaching you. Most within the dream help build and support the dream which allows you to conceive of new knowledge and possibilities, helping you prepare yourself for future events. They are entities within your dream, created by you. In essence, you are their God for they are a figment of your imagination, they are your dream within yourself. But on the other hand, you are you and part of you is composed of your conjurings. Thus people, in turn, are a part of you or, to put it another way, they are a piece of God; they *are* God.

Awakening and coming back to reality, you open your eyes and see the world as you have always known it. And having dreamed of being God, having read of the possibility of a new and different perception, being now aware of your two choices, you will have to choose. Are you going to remain immersed in the philosophical perceptions theism and pantheism generate? Are you going to remain immersed in the perception that you have no significance in reality other than to remain subservient to God because God's size remains in a state of equilibrium?

Or are you going to become immersed in the philosophical perception panentheism generates, that you have a wonderful significance, for you add to the very omniscience of God Itself, thus increasing God's omnipresence and omnipotence? Imagine having such a magnificent purpose. Imagine being equal to God, being God. With such a perception comes the realization that all others are likewise significant. No one is more significant than another. No one is superior to another. No one has the right to subjugate or interfere with the journey of another. We, in fact, have the obligation to protect the journey of all.

However, we scoff at the possibility of improving ourselves through acceptance of such a simple thing as a change in our perception of our significance in reality. We remain God's worst nightmare as we bow our head in the act of submission to our Creator and continue to glorify our Master and sing Its praises.

A Toy

Speculation 2350 A.D.: Journeying thus far has not been easy on our psyche. In 300 short years, we have had to come to terms with the revelation that not only are we imprisoned in a bottle like a bug, but found our ancestry originates from violent social outcasts. The stress on humankind is beginning to show and 2350 is not going to make matters any better for us.

"Quark: n. [coined by Murray Gell-Mann, b. 1929, American physicist] a hypothetical particle that carries a fractional electric charge and that is held to be a constituent of known elementary particles" is the definition presented in Webster's New Collegiate Dictionary. This definition was established forty four years after the birth of the quark's perceptual artist, after the birth of the scientist that is to paint the picture of a quark on a canvas using the medium of words and mathematics. The term quark, the concept quark, becomes an accepted element within our reality.

We have finally confirmed the concept of the quark. Four hundred thirty one years after the birth of the quark's spokesman, scientists have concrete evidence of the quark. Theoretical physicists, quantum physicists, theoretical mathematicians, nuclear physicists, and chaos mathematicians have finally solved the question regarding the long sought after universal building block of life, of physical matter, of the universe. Both mathematicians and physicists have combined their energies in a manner more rewarding than any of them had ever dreamt possible.

We now understand the elementary building block upon which all matter can be created. The universe has now been supplied the simplicity and fundamentals necessary to create all physical matter. A model has been constructed providing the means by which all subatomic particles can be built, including the resultant interactive nuclear forces. We can now theoretically create quarks from energy, elements from quarks, compounds from elements, DNA cells from compounds, tissues from cells, organs from tissues, biological systems from organs, organisms from biological systems. We are on the verge of creating life. Within the short span of five hundred years, we are moving from understanding the structure of a cell to understanding the basic building block of the elements that, in turn, act as the building blocks of life. Surely it is but a question of time before we create life. Imagine us creating life three or four hundred short years from now. Imagine, we will become a god.

All we have to do is put the pieces together. Our thoughts revert to our early youth, to the days of tinker toys. How exciting a time, how exciting to live in an age when we realize how basic we are in structure and how simple in terms of a mechanism.

An unexpected turn of events begins to develop as the excitement of physicists and mathematicians exudes throughout all academia. As fast as the level of excitement over creating rises to a crescendo in the lofty towers of the intellectuals, the morale of the general population, the backbone of society, crashes to a level of despair. The general population doesn't understand the significance of this dramatic new unveiling within our reality. The general population perceives the discovery of building life as a confirmation that we are nothing but a thing built by "something," probably God, as a toy, a means of temporary distraction from Its main thought process and existence. The general population senses that if they can build life, then the process of creation of life must not have been that significant. We are not significant. We begin to see ourselves as a toy, a toy of God. We see ourselves as having no significance. Previously, we saw ourselves as nothing but a slave of God and we were willing to accept that concept, as inferior as it made us feel. The concept of servitude, as low as it placed us on the scale of significance, still allowed us to maintain some sense of dignity, for even a lowly servant has some form of purpose. And thus we were able to cling to some dignity through the hope that we had a purpose to play in eternity, even if it was only to be singing songs of glory to a superior God.

The general population accepted the status of servant because even servants are needed in "heaven," aren't they? But a toy! How can we accept that we are not only inferior to God but, in actuality, just a toy with which God tinkers as It idles away what few empty times It may be able to scrounge together out of Its most certainly busy existence? We lost even the significance of being committed to eternal servitude. We become but a toy with which to tinker and throw away once the novelty is worn off. All humankind, other than a few intellectuals, lose hope of their significance. We continue to stock the shelves, build the infrastructures, grow the food, collect other people's garbage, teach the young, nurse the sick, maintain the very society that supports these intellectuals that have done none other than reduce us from a level of subservience to the level of a trinket, a toy, a construction project intended to give God some form of diversion as It pauses for a moment of relaxation from Its more important business.

All humankind plummets into the depths of despair never before seen. This occurs so swiftly that religions and philosophy have no time to shore up our ego. We enter a state of depression exasperated by the philosophy that we are nothing other than a lowly servant to a glorious God. We are now faced with the concept that existence within reality is reduced to the same common denominator, the same building blocks, as a lowly virus that invades the body. We find that our essence is composed of quarks. We become so emotionally traumatized over being nothing other than a model made from common quarks that we retch and spew the contents of our aggressive nature all over and throughout reality.

We are in a depression so deep that it is questionable if we will be able to pull ourselves out of it and regroup. Civilization is now developed to the point that food, clothing, shelter, health care, recreation facilities, learning centers, support groups have all evolved to a level never before seen in society. We have to work only a few hours a week to keep society humming at top efficiency, but now we find ourselves living in a utopia with no purpose, no hope of being significant. We serve a God, glorify a God, that now has little interest in us, little need of us. We interact with God, who in the long run, only interacts with us as a recreational toy, an interactive mechanism constructed with the Legos of quarks.

Unknown to us, the experiment of the 1980's are about to be played out with the likes of people. In the 1980's, psychologists conducted experiments with rats. The rats were introduced into a utopian environment. They were given everything they needed:

proper diet, optimal temperature and humidity, disease-free environment, recreational devices, ample space, no stress. The rat colony prospered and flourished in the beginning. Over time, however, things began to change. The rat population began to take on a listless tone. As time passed, the rats began to stop reproducing and, eventually, the colony of rats faded away and finally died out altogether as they, producing no offspring, died of natural causes. The rats had lost the will to reproduce, the will to continue life through propagation, and so it seems that humankind has likewise lost its sense of purpose, its sense of significance. We appear to be losing our desire to continue.

What if things had been different? What if panentheism prevailed? If we had perceived ourselves as playing a significant role in reality through which we traveled, if we had seen our significance extend beyond reality into eternity, we would never have lost hope. We would have summarily dismissed the discovery of the quark, the discovery of the universal building block as nothing other than an interesting discovery that had absolutely nothing to do with our significance in reality. We would have seen our significance as being an integral aspect of God.

We are an essential element of God; we exist within a reality located within God. We are none other than a piece of God Itself, traveling reality. Some souls are here to maintain society; some are here to improve society; some are here to move society to a higher level so that others souls may learn and create newness so that God Itself may grow. We take our new knowledge with us when our physical body and mind expire. We reinfuse back into God to become even greater.

We stock the shelves, build the infrastructures, grow the food, collect other people's garbage, teach the young, nurse the sick, maintain the very society that supports the intellectuals that have discovered a new piece of knowledge. We do nothing other than further support the concept that reality is not what is important, but rather, what follows reality is what is important. We understand we have a significant role to play in eternity. God marvelously created us out of universal building blocks of the quark in order to increase Its very essence, in order to grow. God created a tool intended to give

Itself even more significance than It already has. We are an essential piece of important business God must attend to, an important teammate of God's for whom It cheers. Imagine, we have God as a cheering section.

Humankind rises to the heights of ecstasy no sensual pleasure could possibly duplicate, for the pleasure is one of emotional and eternal bliss – not sensual and temporary pleasure. We attain a state of responsibility having purpose beyond reality. We attain a true status of equality for all. We rise to the status of God Itself. We have no higher level to which we can rise. And while rising to this ultimate level, we manage to pull all others with us.

Reality is a place within which God is germinating a seed of optimism. God generates a new philosophy that raises the value of the soul to its ultimate peak, far exceeding any status a lowly servant glorifying God could possible attain. We may find our existence within reality is physically reduced to that of a quark, to the same common denominator, the same building blocks as a lowly virus invading the body; but we, under a new philosophy of who we are and what our function is within reality, recognize that our body is not who we are. We recognize that our essence is, in fact, the soul. We are a piece of God and nothing can reduce the significance of God, the Creator of this reality and, therefore, nothing can reduce the significance of us, of each and everyone of us, of you or I.

Civilization is now developed to the point that food, clothing, shelter, health care, recreation facilities, learning centers, support groups have all evolved to a level never before seen in society. We have to work only a few hours a week to keep society humming at top efficiency and now find ourselves living in a social utopia allowing time to explore and learn in order to expand the very essence of God. We have a purpose. We are significant. We serve God through journeying reality as God. We interact with God, who in the long run, interacts with us. You and I are pieces of God; you and I are in a symbiotic relationship with God; you and I *are* God.

But alas, we are still not ready for the change in perception. We are not ready to accept panentheism and, although we do not succumb to the same fate the rat colony had, we do lose a quarter of all our population before the depression is lifted. Servitude, life, goes on. We become resigned to our perceived fate – we are a servant of a greater being. People are so persistent a creature that we find some peace in a reality of subjugation. We are eternally optimistic because we sense, deep down inside, that we are more than just a toy. We sense, deep, deep down, that we do have significance, and so we continue to move on in time.

Growing

Speculation 2400 A.D.: Equilibrium is a state of remaining the same, an unnatural state of nature. Things may exist in a state of equilibrium for a limited time, but never forever. All things eventually change and there are only two states of change, withering away or growing more significant. 2400 brings us to this realization. For the first time, we see religious institutions, our most comforting bastions, confronted with the irrational concept of God being in an equilibrium state of omniscience, omnipotence, omnipresence. Religious institutions struggle to keep God in a perpetual state of equilibrium because, if God cannot remain constant, then neither can religion. And so philosophy opens its first salvo against the ultimate state of eternal equilibrium. Philosophy takes on God's omniscience.

First, there was God, the omniscient, all-knowing creator. Then there were people, God's underling, God's subservient creation. So it always was and so it shall always be, unless we decide to change it. "It" is the status of us being a subservient creation of God's; it is not a status created by us, it is a status defined by us. If we can define ourselves as such, we can redefine ourselves. We have free will; we have the choice. All we need is confidence in accumulated knowledge, logic, and rationality.

A new war begins, a war of intimidation and desperation, a war of emotions and the threat of our greatest fear – eternal hell. On one side, people use religious institutions to protect the status quo, to avoid change, and protect their personal status through the power of their supposed religious connection with and supposed insight into God. On the other side are the intellectuals, philosophers, down trodden, women, blacks, yellows, and browns, oppressed, impoverished souls delegated to a lower status, males burdened with the sins of their fathers.

And just what is "it?" "It" is merely a perception of who we are. Words are powerful, for they are the tools that act as switches for most of us, switches that shut down the process of thinking, of questioning. Take the word "merely" in the above statement. It is a word that relegates our status to that of mere mortals. Again words, "mere" and "mortals." Words, at the speed of light, propel our brains into a state of shutdown and acceptance as to who we are as individuals. These definitions and perceptions are generated not by religions, but by people of religion. Well-intentioned people yearn to direct humankind into an acceptable behavioral state in order to elevate the status of each individual to a level deserving respect and compassion.

And what has it taken to establish this very concept of the importance of all individuals, the concept of equality? It has taken violence itself. Wars of the past ranging from the Hundred Years Wars, Crusades, WWI, WWII, Cold War to WWIII – the war of abortion and capital punishment, the war over defining "life and "death." They are wars intended to acknowledge through actions the importance of the individual and the individual's journey. The pursuit of raising the status of each individual to an equal status through the violence of war may have been slow but it has been steady. There is undoubtedly a long way to go, but until we begin to challenge our subservience to God, we will always maintain in the back of our minds the concept of subservience. Subservience is a concept that needs total eradication to protect us as individuals and as groups of minorities, women, homosexuals, children, aged, etc., from others attempting to dominate and subjugate us. Subservience is a concept that needs total eradication to protect us from some of the more intelligent life forms in space that may try to dominate us as individuals and as a species.

But the concept of subservience, lower status, worthlessness, cannot be eradicated as long as it exists in any form. This is a radical statement for we perceive ourselves to be subservient to God and that, too, must go for it is the original point of the perpetuation of the concept of subservience. But the concept of our subservience to God will not go down easily.

Who developed our status? Religious institutions and philosophy, as a team, developed our status. When philosophy began to evolve into the realm of thought that questioned our status as an underling of God, religious institutions severed its tie to philosophy and went off on its own, taking with it most of humankind's intellectuals, for even intellectuals fear eternal hell. And with the draining of all but the most daring intellectuals from its ranks, philosophy shriveled up into a small realm of its own that exists only in the ranks, the minds, and the conversations of the most brave of the brave. With the most reckless abandonment, these few ignore the threat religious institutions hold over them, the threat of eternal hell. These people throw caution to the wind in their desire to find answers to questions that haunt them, drive them, consume them. "Who am I, what is my reality, what is my purpose in reality?" These questions apply, not only to themselves, but to all people, to the human race.

How do we finally eradicate the concept of our subservience to God? We do so paradoxically by accepting the concept that God is the most Holy. We do so by finally nailing down our understanding that God is an omniscient, omnipotent, omnipresent being, our Creator, our model of emulation, our Guide to life, the Truth and the Light, our source of comfort, our source of hope, our source of love.

How do we do this without automatically relegating ourselves to an inferior being? The means to do this is laughingly simple. We raise ourselves to the level of God. We understand, through logic, that we are not who we see ourselves to be as we look in the mirror, but rather we must look deep within ourselves. We must look past the surface of what we see. We must look to the very depths of our being, to the essence, to the soul itself. We must look to the core of the machine and there we will see God.

This is a change in perception, a change in religious orientation. This is a change that will generate other changes through a ripple effect so intense, so monumental that nothing will be the same again. Individuals will look at themselves differently; society will see individuals differently; individuals will see each other differently. No longer will we see people as people. We will see others as God; we will look at ourselves as God.

How do we begin to penetrate the armor of religious institutional perceptions regarding humans as subservient to God? We begin by attacking the weak spot in the armor surrounding religious institutions and this can take place when we find the weak point. Can we find this weak point? Certainly. The weak point is obvious. One only has to look at the point being jealously guarded by religious institutions. We must look to the point guarded by religious institutions in as inconspicuous a manner as possible in their attempt to avoid drawing attention to this Achilles' heel. Finding this weak point in the armor is not a case of finding what will allow the termination of religious institutions. It is what will force religious institutions to change their perceptions of us and who we are. Will this destroy religion? By no means, but it will modify a perception of religious institutions. In fact, the change in perception will, as you will see, actually draw us closer to God rather than increase the distance between God and ourselves.

Where is the weak point that religious institutions guard? It lies in the region science has been hammering away at for years. It lies in the region our few and scattered philosophers have been investigating with unrelenting persistence. It lies in the understanding of our universe, our reality, and what it is. It lies in the understanding of just what our purpose is in reality, a purpose which can only be understood when we understand just what reality is.

Science has shown time and again that nothing we have seen in nature exists in the comfort of perpetual equilibrium. Change comes to all things. All things eventually must either grow or wither away. Sunny days give way to cloudy days give way to sunny days. Children come and children go. Glaciers come and go. Mountains rise and erode away. The sun shines but eventually will burn out. The universe expands and will either contract once again or expand into insignificance as its density dilutes itself into infinite nonexistence. All things change.

The concept of us being servants of God is not the exception. It is an idea and is not exempt from the laws of nature, the laws of perpetual change. Nothing stays in a perpetual state of equilibrium, including our perception of ourselves, in spite of what religious institutions may desire. Things either eventually change through growth or things change through erosion. Religious institutions are no different. They cannot wish away the unnatural state of equilibrium just because they do not want to change. Nobody likes change and religious institutions are no exception. They can either accept change and grow or they will erode away as do all things in nature.

Now for the concept of God. Religious institutions defy the laws of nature through professing that God is in a state of equilibrium. This is their Achilles heel, the point they guard jealously in order to avoid change. Their weak point lies in clinging to the concept that God is omniscient, omnipotent, and omnipresent. New perceptions in philosophy indicate that although this is true, it does not imply that God cannot increase Its very essence of all three. Its means of doing so? Traveling within realities using vehicles such as the machines of humans, machines carrying Its essence, Its being, what we know and refer to as the "soul." Souls are portions of God traveling within realities, laboratories isolated from God Itself while at the same time immersed within It. Realities are able to dissolve into nonexistence and thus are able to evolve from nonexistence. The specifics are found in the book, *You & I Together*.

Religion, East and West, for the most part, agrees there is a God and there are people. Both agree that people are subservient to God, inferior to God. Both perceive people as a creation of God, a servant of God. Religious institutions, East and West, attempt to overrule reality, the new concepts science and philosophy are beginning to understand, concepts that do not support the perception that people are subservient, that we have no purpose, that we are insignificant to God. Philosophy is a realm religious institutions have successfully relegated to an outcast existence, for it deals with the abstract. Science is a realm religious institutions have had difficulty holding down, for it deals with our concrete observations and curiosity.

What are some observations of science that raise doubts regarding the perception of us as subservient to God? They are observations such as the primordial atom out of which the universe popped, a bounded universe, time travel, the big bang possibly reversing itself, the possibility of life in space, evolution, antimatter, the symmetry of all things, energy having no symmetry, primary building blocks, out-of-body experiences, the concept of an afterlife, and on and on it goes.

Science opens up the realm of the concrete and philosophy opens the realm of the abstract. Science and philosophy both attack not religion, but the basic perception of religious institutions regarding just who we are. Religious institutions, East and West, desire to overrule the small portion of reality science and philosophy are exposing, an unveiling of who we are, the unveiling of us as God. Religions, East and West, desire to hold onto the perception of us as a subservient being since this will continue to place us in the role of subservience to the church, to religions, to each other.

Imagine we are God. Imagine God being dependent in a small way upon us, upon you, upon me. We would still remain dependent upon God, but now both of us are together in a symbiotic state. We are not the same as God, for God is more omniscient than we are.

To gain a better perspective of this, let's project ourselves beyond earth, our solar system, our galaxy, our universe, our reality, well into the region of God, and look around. As we look, we see a multitude of small bubbles floating around within God. Now let's begin our journey back home. Let's do so in an unusual manner. Let's do so by leaving our body and mind in place and only travel as awareness, a something but not a physical something. As we gaze around, we become aware of many specks floating within God's existence.

Our awareness starts accelerating towards the surface of earth located far beyond our vision. We speed past the specks within God. As we approach a particular speck, we see it is actually four bubbles tied together as balloons. We recognize this as our reality. We recognize our reality as four universes in one, symmetrical and parallel in nature. Our awareness begins the journey into one of these universes and begins to see the emergence of a multitude of galaxies. Our journey then proceeds into one galaxy in particular. Soon, a yellow star appears orbited by a series of planets. The closer we get, the more apparent it becomes that we are headed towards a beautiful blue and white sphere. We pass a large white and gray object appearing to take up a large section of the sky. Our awareness enters the atmosphere and journeys onward until it finally comes to rest within a physical being that now possesses awareness and rationality. This physical being provides our awareness with a sensory means of experiencing the reality, the universe, the galaxy, the star system, the biome, the machine we finally entered. This machine is bestowed with mortality occupied by an awareness maintaining its immortality. People are machines, but the spirit, the soul, and awareness are temporary occupants of the machine, for you and I, our souls, are pieces of God and are predestined to return to God.

God is omnipotent, omnipresent, omniscient but continuously becomes even more so. God grows and thus avoids decay. Even God cannot remain in a constant state of equilibrium. God must either grow or die. This is a new perception, an exciting perception, for we become a part of God. We no longer are a servant of God; we become God. The soul becomes a means by which God enters realities to learn, experience, and grow, and we become a vessel within which God can reside for a limited time. We depend on God for what we call life, awareness. God depends on us for growth. Both depend upon each other, both exist together in a symbiotic state drawing us even closer to God, raising us to the level of God Itself.

We cannot change this, it just is and until we are ready to accept this and redefine ourselves as God, until we are ready to grow up and accept the responsibilities that come with this status, the violence and conflict between us will continue and will accelerate. It will continue because we choose not to accept a redefinition of ourselves. We choose instead to look at some of us as having more importance than others; we choose to perpetuate the perception that we are subservient to God. If we choose not to accept the redefinition of ourselves and accept the responsibility that comes with it, we will continue to see new violence and conflict.

If religious institutions will not submit to change, then violence and conflict will continue and will follow us throughout the millennium. But alas, we and our religious institutions are not ready yet. And so a persistent old companion of ours emerges into a new domain. As we begin our exploration of space in earnest, we take with us the concept of Evil, the Devil, Satan. We carry an affinity for violence and conflict into space as we did into the "new world" centuries ago.

Philosophy has failed to turn us around. Religious institutions wield their power and overrule reality. God remains omniscient in our eyes. Religious institutions, the main bastions clutching to status, inequality, and subservience, are afraid of losing control. Philosophy is not strong enough by itself to change our perception of ourselves. Philosophy is unable to change the flow of history, the flow of our direction into the future. We move on under the weight of subservience, violence, uncertainty, and doubt regarding our true significance. We are afraid to grow. We move on to 2400 only to find ourselves to be another Typhoid Mary.

“Typhoid Mary”

Speculation 2450 A.D.: We have not been able to change our viewpoint regarding our status in relationship to our Creator. We still think we are subservient. Our viewpoint is not to be taken lightly, for we carry it wherever we go, even into the far reaches of space. Unfortunately, when we leave, we do not clean up after ourselves.

Hygiene is not one of our strong points. The environment lacks it. Social interactions lack it. And even our mind, our perception of ourselves, lacks it. Our self-perception is riddled with belittlement, subjugation, violence, feelings of inferiority, perceptions of superiority, judgmental viewpoints, and desire for power and control.

We try, but we just cannot leave violence behind. It follows us wherever we go. We leave it even in places we don’t physically go. We contaminate places we visit not only with robotic capsules but with TV, radio, and microwave messages. Everywhere we go, we leave our viewpoints regarding subservience, ambition for status, and rationalizing violence as a means of advancing one’s status. By 2450, we manage to physically travel within much of near space and are able to send our message to the far reaches of space. We begin to bloom as a flower in the grasp of technology, science, and knowledge. But we stagnate in our concepts of reality, who we are, what our purpose is in reality. Our philosophies begin to wither away as religious institutions become bastions of dogma, as laws of nature governing equilibrium begin to catch up to our stagnation in the perceptions of ourselves and our function within reality.

And thus we enter our new realm and take our first significant step into the dream we have held since we first gazed into the heavens. We have stepped over our first significant threshold since we last stepped on the moon almost five hundred years ago. We are now exploring the planets of our nearest star neighbor, Alpha Century, and have found intelligent life! Granted, not as technologically advanced as ours, and not as intellectually capable as us, but we have found life! Now we know, somewhere out there, we will almost certainly find a life form equal to us, as deserving as us, a life form we can relate to.

Intellectually, the life forms on the planet orbiting Alpha Century are not anywhere near that of ours, but they do approach what we consider to be above the intellectual level of apes. Our curiosity, excitement, and enthusiasm is unbounded. As an extra bonus, we find a rare source of energy in abundance within the planet, never found in abundance anywhere else. Our physicists tell us this source could theoretically provide the means for us to travel the galaxy unfettered by the chains that confine us to our nearest star.

We are caught in a dilemma. We feel the need, the compulsion, to advance into the stars, to explore the near regions of space, but we need the energy source that may make this possible. We need a means of mining this resource but we do not have the means to do so in an unobtrusive fashion. This is not a problem, however, for the life forms we have found are sub-intellectuals. They are only animals intended for our exploitation. Traditional and classical theism tell us that these sub-intellectuals were placed in our region of dominance for the purpose of propelling us into a more glorious status amongst the stars, towards our purpose in reality, populating the universe itself.

We move into the sphere of the new planet with the enthusiasm and self righteousness that accompanied us into the New World back in the 1500's. We enter a period in history which will be known as the beginning of humanity approaching completion of its dreams to step into space, to tame the solar system, to establish themselves as "the" dominant organism in near space. This point in time will likewise be recognized as one of the great points of history, showering glory and status upon us. We bring with us the understanding, the indisputable facts and logic, that if we are a servant of God, then the inhabitants of this planet, with their lower intelligence, are surely intended to be servants of ours, for we are the superior being.

We will be humane about our superiority, though, for we will show them the "way." We will educate and teach them the ways of "right and wrong." We will raise their level of thinking, technology, social structures, social interactions, and morals. We will teach them so they understand and respect the concepts of "good and evil." But that is not all, for we will not only raise them from their depths of ignorance, we will teach them how to enter the gates of heaven and eternity itself. We will give them the secrets to saving their soul and avoiding the pain of eternal hell.

For those who accept the knowledge, we will give them the rewards they deserve while they carry out their lives within reality. We will raise these individuals to the status they have earned. We will make them the leaders of others. They will be granted positions of hierarchy over nonbelievers. Power will be delegated to those who are willing to accept the truth in order to protect the nonbelievers from themselves.

Just as we are placed on a status level as inferior beings below God, just as we place others on status levels of varying degrees of inferiority on earth, we will teach these new life forms the benefits of status, subservience, and superiority. What is good enough for God, a superior being, is good enough for us, and thus we accept our position of subservience. What is good enough for us is only rightly good enough for these new life forms. What *is* good enough for us? Subservience is good enough for us. Why should anyone or any other life form be different? They must accept the concept of God's superiority. They must learn to accept the concept of status. They must learn that humans are God's chosen ones.

At the same time we are enlightening these intellectually inferior life forms into the ways of good and evil, we will show them benevolence by introducing our advanced health care system, our governmental systems, crude forms of technology, and ways to defend themselves from their neighbors. We have so much to teach them, so many better ways for them to live. In return, all we want is some of their resources. We only want some of their metals, minerals, elements, and oh, by the way, some of the potential energy source their planet has in overabundance. That is not asking much in return for all the things we will be giving them. This is but a small compensation when one considers that not only are we giving them technological and social advances way over and beyond what they could possibly develop within their lifetimes, but they are reaping benefits well beyond anything they could ever expect to develop on their own within the next thousand years.

What is even more beneficial to them is the fact that we are teaching the way to gain eternal life. We are giving them the means to gain life everlasting if only they will accept "evil" for what it is and live by the rules of "good." The fight against the Devil, against Satan, against Evil must never be forgotten, must never be relinquished to any degree. Praise God Almighty, praise our Lord, we, your humble servants, worship you and give you thanks. We will carry your word to the farthest reaches of the heavens.

"Blasphemy, blasphemy," you say. It is not blasphemy. It is what occurred in the explorations of the Americas and it is what will occur in the explorations of the heavens, for we have nothing else with which to replace it. We will still be viewing ourselves as servants of God. We will still be seeing God in the light of theism, God as separate from our reality. God has no need for you, for me, other than using us to sing Its praises. Singing praises to a God that is all knowing and thus, by definition, already knows It is the most omnipotent, omniscient, omnipresent being in the universe. We sing praises to a being that has no need of praise. We have an existence for the sole purpose of singing praises that are simply redundant to the being we are praising.

We have no meaning. We are going through motions that have no significance in eternity. We cling to our mortality and fear that our most terrifying nightmare might indeed be true, that we have no significance in the greater picture. And so, to prove otherwise, we continue to protect our concept of status that if some have more significance than others on this earth, in reality, then it is only logical that some would have more significance than others in eternity. Thus, status in eternity becomes part of our reality.

We carry the virus, the disease, of status into the heavens. Typhoid Mary once again rears her head in the annals of humanity, but this time Typhoid Mary is not a person. Typhoid Mary is a species, the species of humankind. Just as we carried small pox into the Americas, so we now carry a new virus into the near reaches of space. We introduce the concept of status into the heavens, status built upon a foundation of judgmental actions, judgmental perceptions of good and bad, good and evil, God and Satan.

We are such glorious creations of God. We refuse to accept, to choose, the new philosophical perception that we act in a symbiotic state with God. We, in our humility and loyalty to a God we have defined, have opted to refuse to choose to raise our status, raise the status of all around us to a higher plane. This plane would reduce violence and conflict to a very, very minimal level, a level so low that to choose it would be the last act of desperation.

We could have made the choice to perceive ourselves as a part of our Creator, a perception we could carry with us into the heavens, a perception we could have brought to the planet of Alpha Century. We could have made our first contact with intelligent life as a healthy entity. Instead, we come crippled and dying with the disease of status, the disease of violence, the disease of subservience. We are sick and carrying disease because we choose not to change one simple thing, our perception of reality and our place within it. We choose to remain subservient to a Creator that needs us, to a God that, as an entity within this reality, yearns for an understanding of a significant purpose to give Its daily struggles meaning.

The sadness lies not in our pathetic nature nor in what we do to ourselves, for we choose to do so. The sadness lies in the fact that we will carry our inferiority complex into the heavens and spread it like a raging disease to life forms we will encounter just as we introduced new diseases to the Americas. This is the sad part of our journey into the heavens, for these life forms have no choice in the matter. We will not be consulting them before we make contact; we will inevitably make contact that will unavoidably spread our disease, our contaminant of status and subservience.

When will we be ready to change our perception? When will we be ready to accept panentheism? Perhaps when we discover intelligence comparable or superior to our own, and that will surely occur in the not too distant future.

Twins

Speculation 2500 A.D.: Science has long acknowledged the existence of the universal sound known as "Om." Now at the turn of the half millennium, science has established the cause of this sound and when it originated.

Science has undoubtedly determined that the universal sound, the energy emission located everywhere in our universe, has as its source the explosion of the "primordial atom." The "big bang" theory is correct. Science, through the use of new biomolecular computers, has also determined that the universal noise, acting as a faint background of all deep space energy emissions received on the earth, comes from not one, but two energy sources. The near uniformity of energy dispersal has provided computer scientists, using much improved artificial intelligence of biomolecular computers, to establish and run a mock-up model of the historic explosion of our primordial atom.

With this final proof came the establishment of when the explosion occurred. Science now knows for certain that our universe is not only expanding but when and where the event of expansion began.

The second energy factor, which is mixed in with the background noise caused by the explosion that created our universe, is energy being emitted from the only turbulent region located on the universe's boundary. Upon analysis, this second energy factor theoretically provides the proper magnitude of energy to account for the anomalies within the universal noise, "Om." This energy release matches the theoretical physicists' projections of what would be produced if our universe, which is composed of matter, came into contact with a universe composed of antimatter.

The pattern of emission matches the mathematical models of two Klein bottle universes in contact. It appears that our universe has a twin of antimatter. It appears that not only does our universe have an exterior but, through the symmetry of matter and its opposite, antimatter, could theoretically be tied to a parallel universe.

Two universes which, upon merging, would reduce everything of substance, all matter and antimatter, into pure energy. It appears that the substance of our universe has only temporary substance.

Two new astounding characteristics of our universe have emerged from these studies. One, our universe has a starting date and two, our universe is most probably attached to a second Klein bottle, a second universe separate from ours but tied to ours.

Not only have we become trapped within a temporary bottle, but now we find that the bottle within which we exist is not unique. We have not only lost our perception of being unique, we have lost the perception that our universe is unique. These are very troubling discoveries indeed for our ego, our yearning to be unique and essential within the concept of eternity.

Philosophy and religions have their work cut out for them. We know that we developed in a universe which was not always in existence. We now know the date of origination of the universe. We realize we were predated by "something" else. We are not unique nor essential to what existed before. It logically follows that whatever preceded us will follow us. Humans cannot be the ultimate of beings. Religions and philosophy come to the same conclusion: we are not essential to the existence of the universe we occupy. We are expendable; we are an insignificant being in the vastness of the universe and what lies beyond.

Coming to terms with the realization that our reality had a beginning, was predated by something else, is not easy. Understanding and accepting that our reality is accompanied by a second, parallel universe composed of antimatter makes matters even worse. Now all material substance can be reduced to pure energy. We hang tight and cling even tighter to the concept that we must have been created to glorify our Creator. Why else? Theistic religions are strengthened. Our faith in our subservience, our lower status, is intensified and with it comes the further entrenchment of the conviction that we were created by something greater. A Creator has created status levels of significance for all things in the universe: rocks, grass, trees, insects, snakes, fish, birds, dogs, biomes, planetary bodies, humans. We are at the top of it all. We are only one step below the magnificence of God. We are willing to fight to maintain our status. We become even more united as a species and agree we will join in a united front to secure that status against any intelligent life form we may encounter. We are on a quest to spread our influence, the influence of God, throughout the heavens.

Hidden within this system of hierarchy of significance are subsets of status. We have status subsets of our own of color, gender, sexuality, intelligence, religious affiliations, physique, ad infinitum. We know our place in society. We unite on the surface, but quietly below the surface, we compete to move whatever minority group we belong to a higher level of status.

We use the resources God provided to expand our influence throughout the universe. We roll in turmoil beneath the surface of tranquillity. We feel the urgency of time, drive for the heavens in search of other intelligent life forms, which must be shown "the truth and the light." How glorious a purpose; we are on a mission of establishing a choir of multiple life forms to sing the praises of a Creator that has given the precious gift of life and, in return, expects nothing other than appreciation. We are on a mission to create a choir that will raise its voice as one until heaven resonates from one end of its boundaries to the other.

We stand at the right hand of God. We are undoubtedly God's most loyal servant and the religious, political, legal, corporate, academic leaders, who have lead humankind to this level of glory for God, will surely reap the benefits as they enter God's Kingdom. The leaders of humankind expect to have others follow them through those gates, looking up to them in appreciation for their influence in having the gates of heaven flung open for all the loyal servants. The leaders believe they will reap the fruits of their labor in eternity to follow. They believe they are to be held in high esteem, placed upon pillars of adoration, as the masses group beneath them singing their praises in addition to God's throughout eternity to follow.

Oh the glory of it all; onward to the heavens! The glory of eternity awaits you. Push for the development of the mines on our beautiful silvery moon, the heavenly object that has comforted us in the dark of the night for the last ten thousand years. Push for the development of the first signs of our presence on a planetary body to be seen from earth. Push for the creation of a new mountain on the moon built from the lunar mine extractions representing our advancement into the heavens. Exploit the tundras, deserts, mountains, rivers, streams of earth. Oh – they are already stripped of their cleanliness and substance? They already have had their beauty and form desecrated? No matter, it was for a good cause. Let's not look back; let's move on. There is plenty more of the same in other places of the heavens. Let's move on to the planets and other stars in our near vicinity. Forward, God awaits, glory awaits. And what of the future children to come? They will do as we did. They will provide for themselves for we will teach them well the ways of independence.

It is the way it has always been, and it is the way it will always be, for we have no options, no alternatives. History dictates that it shall be so. History dictates. What of the present? Can we not change the direction of history?

The universe was predestined to come into existence and predestined to terminate, but other than that, the universe is not in a predestined state. The universe can evolve in a unique manner directed by traveling souls within the confines of the Klein bottle the universe occupies. We exist within the universe as much a free agent of predestination as the inner state of the universe itself. We, in the present, are the ones to set the direction for the future. The past does not set the direction of the future. The past is gone. We, you and I, set the direction of the future. But in order to change this direction, we have to stop acting as others did in the past. We have to stop thinking of ourselves in the same way others in the past thought of themselves.

Presently, we perceive ourselves to exist for the purpose of glorifying the Creator. There is, however, another option: panentheism. We could just as well perceive ourselves as entities existing not as subservients of the Creator but as equals with It. Our purpose is to help God, ourselves, grow through the process of traveling reality. Some are to add to God's growth directly; others are to support, build, maintain, groom, elevate a growing society that will allow new growth for God. All of us will become fully aware of how we helped God, ourselves grow through our actions in reality after our reinfusion back into God, once again becoming a part of our Creator after our journey through reality is completed.

But who is to say that the perceptions presently developed by human sources are correct? If one perception may be correct, why not another? And if the present day perception of theism is inadequate to explain observed and inferred events within our present reality, if the present day perception is inadequate and lacks the scope to guide us as we confront new problems regarding our role within the universe, then why not modify our perceptions of ourselves to fit the expanded knowledge and adventures that continually confront us?

Why must our philosophy regarding what reality is and our logical function, the reason for our existence within reality, remain stagnant? Why do we have to protect the sacredness of all the principles of theism or pantheism? Why can't we modify the concept that we are servants of God and become a piece of God instead? Why can't we modify the concept that God is a separate entity of reality and allow our reality to become a small piece of God?

Two changes are needed in our perception that would expand our purpose. The first change requires us to accept that although God is all-knowing, all-present, and all-powerful, It can become even more so. The second change requires us to accept that we are a part of God sent to reality to help God, ourselves, grow. These changes would alter the perception of reality itself and would generate other changes for the better, for they would cause us to act more like God. After all, isn't this what we have always been trying to accomplish?

This is not a discussion in futility. We do have an option regarding our philosophical perception of ourselves and of our function within reality. Whatever the potential trauma may require, panentheistic perception would allow us to rationalize, accept or confront potentially traumatic physical events in a positive manner. Whatever incident may occur that would rock the very confidence of all humankind in terms of our significance within reality can be faced confidently and proudly with the right perception.

Theism, pantheism or panentheism is a choice, our choice, your choice. The fork in the road is not made up of scientific discoveries. The fork in the road has not changed. The fork in the road is a choice between philosophical perceptions.

But our journey is still not done. We are only halfway through the new millennium and we have much to discover within the heavens as well as within the mind. Our journey continues under the old philosophy of subservience to God, inferiority to God. But it is only 2500 and the fun has just begun.

Contact

Speculation 2550 A.D.: The second half of the millennium begins with a surprise visit from space. We are about to be confronted with something new. We are about to encounter violence from an alien life form. We are about to embark upon violence for species survival. This is not something new. We have written about it for a thousand years, but now it is really happening.

Extraterrestrials come to us for the first time. To our surprise, they are not that much more advanced than we as a human species. In fact in many ways, other than technologically, they are more primitive. Their primal behavioral motivation seems to be the same as ours, oriented around subjugation and domination of species with which it comes into contact.

The earth, however, is well-populated, armed, and ready for just such an encounter. Nations are united as a whole under the United Nations to deal with just such an encounter. As a united species, we will have no problem holding our own and maintaining our uniqueness as a species.

We are truly now a theistic species, united cohesively, held together by the understanding of our purpose in reality and what reality is. We understand the we are the servant of God, a creation of God, and as such, have clearly defined status levels for all. Social status, occupational status, economic status, racial status, gender status, sexual status, to name just a few, are all well-defined and we have been placed accordingly into our own particular status niche.

Society has been honed to an impressively efficient mechanism capable of granting satisfaction of our most personal desires. Society has found a means of providing full satisfaction to both our bodies and minds, thus drawing us together as a total unit working for the glory of God. We have finally found contentment in our pursuit to fulfill our purpose in reality: the purpose of being a loyal and accepting servant, subservient, of God's.

Humankind is organized and well-directed by both government and religious institutions. Humankind is prepared and running at full efficiency, molded into a lean and mean machine.

First contact has given us an understanding of the primal objective of these new life forms. We fully understand their objectives of subjugation and dominance. Being prepared, we have no doubt that realizing our cohesiveness, they will come away impressed and respectful of our resolve and decide the best thing for both of us is to open up peaceful and mutually beneficial contacts, trade, and technology exchange.

Our first contact has been successful and just as we anticipated. Trade, technological exchange, and embassy establishments have been opened up quickly and with mutual understanding.

As time passes, our society begins to show some stress and disgruntlement. Lower levels of our status system begin to show some discontent and rumored reports begin to surface of some people acting covertly and in conjunction together as they pursue personal gain for themselves. Society's ability to provide a sensual hedonistic mechanism for all is beginning to show it has possible weak points.

The new life forms seem to be attempting to undermine our efficient system of a just and benevolent social status arrangement that has taken 500 years to perfect, a system that has been established through patient negotiation with various social segments of society. This fair status system puts people in their correct place.

The new life forms may be attempting to subvert the system by appealing to the very motivational drives the system itself provides, penetrating the lines of social demarcation with the invisible weapon of greed. Who would have thought more power, greater wealth, racial superiority, religious bias, and gender issues could ever have resurfaced again? These were all issues relegated to the ashes of history. The conflict of status was resolved, accepted, and put behind us. Through understanding and accepting our old, stable philosophy and theology regarding subservience to God, we accepted our natural status of being the highest level that exists under God. Society was finally able to imitate perfection, portraying equally acceptable status systems for all. Using skilled arbitration, keen negotiation, theistic models, advanced judicial systems, and intricate give and take for all socially developed levels of status, we had formulated a social order whose equilibrium was equilibrium personified.

Who would have thought blacks would have risked their new status in the hopes of gaining even more status through aligning with this inhuman black life form? Blacks now seek a new position of status working in conjunction with the earth invaders and seek to subjugate other races just because they have the same color as the extraterrestrials.

Who would have thought Muslims would have gravitated to extraterrestrials just because they landed in Mecca? Muslims have professed the equality of religions for 300 years but are now seeking a new ally to rekindle their desire to spread "the word" as they see it. Muslims seek to have Mecca as the central point for all humankind.

Who would have thought power-hungry whites would sell out their own race in order to personally gain more power through subjugation? Society had already negotiated safe and dependable levels of power for them that would be theirs for life. Whites use the very power levels society had granted them to negotiate their own deals, to expand their present powers to even newer and grander levels of power. How could they be so insensitive to the needs of others?

Society is breaking down; social groups are beginning to conflict with each other. We are beginning to seek at the expense of others what is best for ourselves and are once again fighting amongst each other to satisfy our own desires. We are reverting to the primal instinct of sensual hedonism. History is once again repeating itself.

We are allowing ourselves to become subjugated by a devious life form intent on dominating and subjugating others. Through the refusal to raise ourselves up to a new level of importance, a new level of significance, we have allowed history to repeat itself at our expense. This is not a new event in the annals of history, it is the same old song being sung to the same old tune, the tune of inferiority with words of superiority. We naturally carry this concept into our social, religious, governmental, educational, and philosophical realms.

This is an unbreakable pattern of history as long as we continue to view ourselves as an underling of God. Under this perception, we will continue both as individuals and small groups to seek short term rewards at the expense of others. This pattern cannot change because nothing has changed. We cannot change our historical patterns without changing what causes historical actions – our perception of ourselves. If we change our perception of ourselves, then historical patterns would change.

Let's take the same situation above and rerun it based upon a new perception of ourselves. Let's run it based upon our equality to God. Not God, but a portion of God having created reality for a reason, traveling reality as a soul within the machine of our bodies, and using our minds as the computer terminal.

Now we are operating under the premise that we are all traveling for the same purpose. We all have a purpose in reality and are equal. Everyone's journey contains the soul of God and may not be desecrated or inhibited for they all add to the omniscience, omnipotence, omnipresence of God Itself.

Now the event can be rerun with surprising results. Extraterrestrials come to us for the first time. We are a united species and are ready for just such an encounter. We will have no problem holding our own and maintaining our uniqueness as a species.

We are united as a cohesive unit held together by the understanding of our purpose in reality and what reality is. We understand the we are a portion of God and as such, have a clearly defined purpose of increasing the very omnipotence, omnipresence, omniscience of God, of all beings with souls. We have thus opened up society to all, recognizing that our essence is not the body nor the mind, but the soul. We have blended panentheism into religion, philosophy, society, and individuality.

As such, society has reevaluated its perception of the environment and recognizes it as the playground, work environment, laboratory, resting place for God. Society, with this new perception, has cleaned up the environment for the benefit of all living today and to come, for they all are pieces of God. Our environment is as clean and sparkling as the blue and white atmosphere the new life forms entered.

Seeing that the new life forms are black in color, we send our most skilled black emissaries to lead because we know our past history and are well aware that this new life form may not have as expanded a mindset regarding their own perceptions of the status of other life forms within reality as we have.

Society has been honed to an impressively efficient mechanism for granting all people the latitude to pursue their own journeys, fulfillment of their own souls, God's journey. Society has fully accepted and incorporated the concept of equality of all people through the model of our equality to God. The concept of violence is one held in abhorrence. We have finally found contentment in our pursuits to fulfill our purpose in reality. Humankind is organized and well-directed by both government and religion, prepared and running at full efficiency. Humankind has been molded into a lean and compassionate machine.

First contact has given us an understanding of the primal objective of these new life forms. We understand this new life form is philosophically oriented around subservience to the creator of reality, rather than panentheism with equality on a level with the creator of reality. We have been there. We fully understand their objectives of subjugation and dominance. Being prepared, we have no doubt that realizing our cohesiveness, they will come away impressed and respectful of our resolve and decide the best thing for both of us is to open up peaceful and mutually beneficial contacts, trade, and technology exchange.

Our first contact has been successful and just as we anticipated. Trade, technological exchange, and embassy establishments have been opened up quickly and with mutual understanding.

As time passes, our society becomes even more efficient and our journeys become even more fruitful. The primal instincts of the extraterrestrials begin to surface. Seeing no results in their efforts to penetrate our perception of ourselves as portions of God, the extraterrestrials begin to show restlessness. They become leery of our obvious acceleration beyond them in terms of all areas of social, religious, governmental, educational, and philosophical realms. We hold fast to our principles, for there is no logical higher level of spirituality to which we can ascend.

In their failure to divide us, the extraterrestrials decide to make a hostile move to physically subjugate humankind and thus expand their power and wealth. Violence is necessary to protect the rights of all rational life forms throughout the universe – all live forms with souls to travel reality as free spirits seeking their spiritual fulfillment.

We take up arms as a cohesive, united front, not just for our species, but for the rights of other species existing today and for those to come. We have a battle cry never heard before, "To battle, for God, for ourselves, for all living creatures!" Humankind, one hundred billion strong, united on land, under the oceans, upon the moon, under the mountains of Mars, and into space itself. We work in full cooperation with others as equals, connected with each other as entities of one species through the soul itself. We fight for the cause of protecting our rights and the rights of others. We fight with the knowledge that although we may lose the battle, the war will never be forgotten, for our actions will follow us into eternity itself. Our actions will become not only a memory we will live with in reality, but our actions will become engraved into the awareness of God. We will be able to relive this memory over and over again with pride because of our universal motivation.

We follow our instincts and drive to maintain panentheism, spiritual hedonism. We are a worthy entity, indeed. We are worthy to explore space, to represent earth, to represent God, for we are a piece of God.

History has taken a new turn. History now recognizes the equality of all rational beings – a true equality through a new perception. We are God. Equality of all souls throughout the universe exists through a symbiotic relationship of souls and God.

Society stands strong, social groups unite with each other, we seek what is best for ourselves, as long as it is best for all souls of God. We fight shoulder to shoulder with each other to maintain the right of all souls to seek spiritual hedonism. As a unit, we refuse to allow subjugation by a life form intent on domination. Humankind, by raising itself up to a new level of importance and significance, has prevented history from repeating itself at everyone's expense.

This is a new event in the annals of history; it is a new song being sung to a new tune of equality. History has now been written with our conception of equality to God, which only naturally carries itself into the concepts of social, religious, governmental, educational, and philosophical realms. We changed history through choice, through a new perception of ourselves. We expanded our views to incorporate all souls traveling the universe. We accepted ourselves as an integral part of reality. We are a peaceful and respectful entity of space.

A choice, being made by us, allows us to respect our uniqueness as we encounter life forms wishing to change, subjugate, dominate, divide, and compromise us. We seek to fulfill our purpose as God traveling reality – a new and admirable beginning for us as we journey the heavens. We are a spiritual entity using a total collective effort in order to remain unique individuals with purpose. We use a collective effort to protect not only our individual journeys now and in the future, but the journeys of all souls. We accept panentheism.

Such a difference! If only we would accept a new perception for ourselves.

Quadruplets

Speculation 2600 A.D.: We encounter half of an old nursery rhyme:

One Klein,
Two Kleins,
Three Kleins,
Four. . .

This nursery rhyme holds much significance to humankind. On the internal surface of our own reality, our own Klein bottle, Klein bottle number one, three anomalies appear. We discovered the first anomaly back in 2500. Now we prove what we had always known in our heart. The universe is based upon symmetry. Multiple parallel universes do exist.

Upon elaborate exploration of our own Klein bottle's inner surface, we have found a surface so elusive, no matter or energy ever comes in contact with it. The interior boundaries of the surface are mapped not by actually coming into contact with the surface, but rather by finding the very outer limits one can penetrate – limits describing the shape of the Klein bottle's surface itself. It is a beautiful surface. Its precision and degree of predictability are all the proof we need to realize that, although we may exist in a bottle, we do not exist in any ordinary bottle. Initially, no one was able to find imperfection anywhere on the perfectly smooth skin.

Then came the discovery of one imperfection, a location of such violent activity that at first astronomers, physicists, and theoretical mathematicians had absolutely no idea what could cause this turmoil on such a tranquil surface. This first chaotic, turbulent anomaly was discovered a hundred years ago in 2500. It is now widely accepted that this, in fact, is a distortion created by a reality, a companion Klein bottle, composed of antimatter and energy coming in contact with our reality, our Klein bottle. There is now little doubt in the minds of scientists that our reality, our universe, has a traveling companion. We exist alongside a parallel universe.

Now this one irregularity, this one anomaly, on the surface of our Klein skin is joined by a second. This second anomaly appears to have dissolved a portion of the Klein's surface, an opening through the Klein surface. Alas, the prefect Klein skin wasn't as perfect as we thought.

On first examination, it was assumed that a hole existed in the reality we occupied! It was thought we had an exit to our universe! We, once again, would be able to travel throughout the infinite. Our dream of infinite realms for us to explore seems about to be reignited. We had found a doorway.

We, being claustrophobic creatures, may not be as confined as we had anticipated. Our dreams are once more sparked by our age-old desire to believe that we could have infinite realms to conquer. We would be able to reconstruct our goal of being the ultimate servant for an all powerful, all knowing, all present entity.

This unexpected discontinuity on the surface of the boundary was unusually elusive to scientific detection due to the fact that it doesn't exist, for "it" is nothing. "It" is a hole in the skin of the Klein bottle. "It" is bounded by randomly undulating sides, which surprisingly mirror the sides of the first anomaly found on the surface of our universe's Klein skin. The first anomaly proved to be a contact with a second universe, a second Klein bottle composed of antimatter.

The new anomaly on the surface of the boundary of our universe proves to be troubling to scientists, however, for it opens up a surprising possibility. It opens up the possibility of the existence of a third reality traveling in conjunction to our own. This reality may be composed of the opposite, the missing symmetry to energy. It appears to be a contact with anti-energy. Anti-energy had long been considered a possibility, but theoretically impossible. It had long been documented that matter and antimatter contacts lead to the annihilation of both matter and antimatter and the resultant product was energy. As Einstein had modeled hundreds of years ago, energy was just a less complex form of matter. Thus, things are continually reduced to their simplest state, the state of pure energy.

If anti-energy did exist, it could never exist in our universe, for it would instantly come into contact with energy and the two would reduce themselves to a simpler state, the simplest of all states for concrete concepts – the state of awareness, or in this case since there is no awareness, the state of nothingness, a vacuum. In more simplistic terms, one might say total annihilation, a void.

There it is in its stark nakedness, a void as the essence of our reality. We encounter again and again the concept of our insignificance because we will not change our perception of what reality is and what part we have to play in eternity. We are afraid to face the responsibility that comes with a perception of significance. We continue to reek havoc with violence, trauma, concepts of relative worth, superiority to others, inferiority to God.

We find comfort in the cloud of insignificance that had been persistently hovering over us. This cloud had been gradually descending upon us and immersed us in its fog of blackness. This black cloud hovered over us for the last six hundred years and now appears to have magically dissipated.

Our conflict with dominating extraterrestrials had taken its toll. The reality check of encountering other intelligent life forms took its toll on our psyche, for it had put us into a state of being just another one of many intelligent life forms.

When we added this to the discovery that we were confined within a type of container we could never leave, the overall effect was to beat our psyche into an inferiority complex we were only able to counter with a turn towards an aggressive, nasty disposition. This compensation factor made us a very unpleasant species with which to come into contact. We were determined to prove ourselves through power and forced subjugation as a means of demonstrating that we were significant. We were subjugating the universe to prove our virility to others, to ourselves, and especially to God.

Now, however, new hope is rising and beginning to rekindle our age-old tendency towards compassion and tolerance. It appears that we are not confined within a bottle, for an opening is present, a way out, a way of expanding the boundaries for exploration. And with this expansion in our perception of our limits comes an expansion in our perception of our need to be accepting and tolerant of other beings in reality. A giving attitude, a willingness to share in the glory of discovery and the approval of God, for there is enough praise from God to go around for everyone. The universe is, once again, no longer finite. The universe is infinite.

Perceptions are important to the individual's, the total species' mental state. Perceptions of confinement lead to perceptions of limits, which translate into inferiority and superiority concepts within the mind. Confinement leads, in fact, to the very concept of inferiority and superiority relationship between the individual and our Creator, a concept that doesn't filter down but rather pours down onto the very bottom levels of society.

Unfortunately, we were not and are still not ready to accept a new perception for ourselves, the perception that we have a very important role to play regarding eternity. We are not ready to accept that we are important to God. We are not ready to accept that we are a means by which God grows, a means by which God avoids the impossible state of eternal equilibrium, a means by which God avoids the only other alternative – wasting away into nonexistence.

And so it is that we, once again, throw ourselves into a state of despair. Through our vast abilities of ingenuity, we find that a third anomaly, a second hole, exists on the Klein skin. Three anomalies lead cosmologists to the conclusion that although we exist within a Klein bottle, our universe is not alone. Rather, our universe has three companions. Including our own, that makes four Klein universes traveling together as a single entity. Our universe travels in time with three other parallel universes. The three anomalies are proof of the existence of our universe passing through. . ., we know not what. Three anomalies are unexpected occurrences on the very surface of the skin of our universe.

One anomaly is on the Klein skin, a circle with dynamically undulating sides displaying turbulence and violence created by the spectacular interaction of matter and antimatter in constant contact. This contact has the resultant production of a constant emission of energy as the two realities annihilate each other and reduce each other to a simpler form – energy.

The second anomaly is on the Klein skin, a circle with dynamically undulating sides displaying a hole, an opening penetrating the very fabric of the Klein skin, a fabric defining our reality to be finite with a hole. Have we found a doorway to infinity? A break in the fabric of the Klein jacket means we can expand our perception of the size of reality. We are inflated by the idea that the degree of our influence has no bounds. We are elated, optimistic, excited about our ability to roam infinity and bring infinite glorification to God.

A third anomaly is found right where it was expected to be if, in fact, our reality is tied to three others, if our reality is just one of four. Our optimism, elation, and excitement are shattered just as they were falsely built up. A third anomaly, a second hole, exists right where it should be if anti-energy, the symmetry to energy, exists. A third anomaly closes off the concept of infinity once again.

Three anomalies and four universes exist. Our universe is made up of matter/energy. The second universe is made up of antimatter/energy. The two, if united, reduce themselves to nothing but energy. A third universe is made up of matter/anti-energy. The fourth universe is made up of antimatter/anti-energy. Universes three and four, if united, reduce themselves to nothing but anti-energy.

Finally and most depressingly, if the energy and anti-energy products unite, it reduces all that remains into a state of awareness only, nothing concrete, nothingness. And so it would be, so it could be, that all we conceive could be reduced to nothing. We are, once again, brought to despair regarding our significance. The cloud of insignificance and depression reemerge more black than ever, hovering and descending, but with a speed and imminence frightening beyond our wildest dreams. Our fear is one of complete annihilation.

We are forced into our age-old identity crisis regarding our own significance in reality by the concept that reality is "nothing at all." We expand our influence through the farthest reaches of space. We are made in the image of God and are capable of dissolving into the simplest state, the state of nothingness. We fight the resultant conclusion that if, in fact, we mirror God, then God images us. Therefore, if we can be reduced to nothing, than what of God? It is too ego-shattering to even contemplate.

In the depths of despair, we cling to old perceptions that cannot keep up with what reality has revealed. We find letting go of the old and embracing new perceptions of just who we are, to be too difficult. We have built a social structure with a life of its own, a social structure permeated to its very depths with the concept coming from our past, the concept of self-preservation. Social structures are so intent on maintaining their own existence that they check us at every move we make to change our perception of reality. Perceptual changes are needed to allow us to move to a new level of understanding, a rationality that would supersede any destructive element nature could throw in our path.

We persist in choosing to hang onto all the old philosophical principles of theism and pantheism rather than meld the two into the universal concept of panentheism, a philosophy capable of becoming a truly universal philosophy for not only humankind but for all other intelligent beings we might encounter through our travels in reality. Panentheism is a philosophy capable of giving a vision so broad, we would be capable of withstanding the terrifying concept that we could be confined in a limited bottle, a Klein bottle, imprisoned for eternity under the old philosophy. We could rise to a multitude of glorious heights under the philosophy of panentheism.

We continue, however, to go down the mountain into the depths of despair created by subservience rather than climb into the glorious heights of mingling as an equal with God Itself. We are going in a downward direction because going downhill is easier. We are looking at the ease of the short run rather than the glory of the long run. Sitting at the doorway of 2650, we are unable to pass through the doorway of change.

A Doorway

Speculation 2650 A.D.: We grab hold of our emotions. We begin to examine the violent spot located on the walls of the prison of our reality. The concept of us going through the two empty doorways leading to other Klein realities composed of anti-energy is farfetched. Any messages sent in the form of matter or energy would be annihilated before it could even get through these two doors, these two holes penetrating the walls of our own Klein bottle.

However, it is not as absurd to begin imagining passing through the first anomaly found on the Klein surface of our reality. This anomaly, at first glance, would appear to be the least likely to be accessible, but that was before we understood the full scope of the model of four parallel universes comprising the whole. Being made of matter and energy, we could never inject our presence or anything resembling a creation of ours into the two parallel universes composed of anti-energy since anything we create must be some form of matter/energy substance. We know that energy of any form, including matter in an energy-based reality, would simply dissolve into nothingness once it came into contact with either matter/anti-energy reality or antimatter/anti-energy reality.

We grab onto the faint glimmer of hope regarding our ability to project our influence outside our own reality through what appears to be the least likely doorway, the doorway on the Klein surface obstructed by violence itself – a concept with which we are well acquainted, a concept with which we are well equipped to deal. So we continue to roam the deep ends of space as we develop the means of sending messages, transmissions of energy through the doorway cluttered with turbulence into the new frontier of a second reality.

Imagine doubling our knowledge every ten years. This factor, within two thousand years, led us from the primitive state of the Roman empire to the voyage into space and walking the moon. Doubling all of our knowledge every ten years has, during the third millennium, accelerated to doubling all of our knowledge in a span of less than every five years. In less than seven hundred years, this leads to the concept of actually communicating with another intelligence within a wholly different, parallel universe.

We realize, however, that even with the aid of knowledge from a second reality combined with our knowledge of our own reality, we almost certainly could not find a way out of our limited existence. The question of the millennium becomes, "Why would a creator place rational beings within prison walls?" We are angry and incensed that our Creator could be so insensitive. Hadn't we willingly placed our significance in the concept of subservience in order to show our Creator gratitude? All we wanted was to be second on the ladder of importance. How can confinement within a finite reality possibly reinforce the concept that we are God's favored servant? How can confinement to even two finite realities solidify our belief that we are second in the line leading away from God?

But we are the eternal optimist and see conquering another, a second reality, as a new beginning. We, once again, pour our heart, intelligence, and soul into developing a means of breaking through into a second parallel universe, a companion reality to our original reality. As the research moves ahead with full force, the ethical and philosophical debates begin to heat up. What right do we have to enter another reality when we cannot even travel through our own in a manner with which we feel proud?

Everywhere we go, there is conflict, violence, abuse. Wherever we travel, the environment becomes scarred, polluted, and barren. We travel in space leaving a significant trail of debris, subjugation, and sense of arrogance. We flaunt our dominance, implant our concept of superiority, and infect all others with the disease of the need for power. Life is no better now than at the turn of the last millennium. What we had then, we still have; the difference is that we have a lot more of it because we have carried it with us as we penetrated almost every part of our reality, either physically or through some form of energy intrusion.

We see ourselves as noble creatures as we seek to resurrect our failing sense of significance generated from finding that we exist within a single, limited reality. We are so egotistical we would even consider entering another reality and contaminating it with our presence. We look around and see how we affect our own reality. Our physical reality is torn apart by our refusal to accept a significance for ourselves more meaningful than that of being subservient to another, and so we work to spread the name, glory, and knowledge of a greater power, a power having no need of us. This perception leads to the belief that the ends, spreading the glory of God, is justified by the means, using and abusing others and the environment through violence and intimidation. One would think nothing could be worse than this. One should, however, never underestimate our creativity. We have gone one step further. Worse than the physical contamination is our ability to implement emotional contamination. We cling to our perceptions of ourselves as being of no value to our Creator other than being a glorified instrument to sing Its praises. As such, we cling to the concept of being inferior to It. This, in turn, leads to the infectious concepts of subservient, individual worth of one over another, guilt, self abuse due to perceptions of having little value, letting others abuse one's environment, using the present to steal from future generations, accepting intimidation, self abuse, appeasement, and on and on. And we become the carrier.

We continue to work as fast as we can while the token debate rambles on regarding our right to spread, to contaminate, a virgin reality. If only we would elevate our perceptions of ourselves, we might actually elevate the level of our behavior. What's the rush? Recognizing that we are not an insignificant servant of a Creator, but rather a significant element necessary for the very growth of our Creator would give us an entirely different perspective regarding our own behavior. The new perspective would lead us out of being confined within our own reality and into the reality that lies beyond our universe. The new perspective would lead us to serious internal reflection before encroaching upon another reality.

We would do more than just perform some token debate before possibly doing damage to a reality created by "something" for a reason. We might decide to first begin to like ourselves and what we do before infecting another reality with our presence. Imagine working to like who we are, what we do, and what we conceive our function and purpose in reality to be before infecting other realities.

It is too late to go back in time and take on this task before infecting the outer reaches of our reality with this decision to like ourselves. Near space was contaminated long ago by the confused, violent, self-serving entity of humankind and far space was unable to hold back the tide of our conception of subservience.

In our desire to lift the cloud of insignificance, we do not understand that all we have to do is accept a different perception of who we are and why we exist, accept a perception of panentheism. Such a simple little concept; we are here for a significant reason. We are here to help God, the creative force that initiated the creation of the four parallel universes comprising our total physical reality.

Panentheism is a concept that supersedes any calamity we could possibly face, for once each soul added its newness to God, it could never be undone. Once newness was added to God, God would have increased in greatness to a new level of significance and even the confinement to a specific finite universe could not eradicate the fact that God had grown. The implosion of a set of four parallel universes back into nothingness would have no effect on reducing God to less significance, for as long as God keeps growing, It will not wither away. The consequences of our acceptance of our significance in reality lies in the startling and radical understanding that once we accept our own personal significance within this context, we have no other rational option but to accept the personal significance of all others. We would have no choice but to accept that our own soul is no more significant than another.

We will never accept our own unimaginable significance as long as we maintain the perception that we are subservient to anything, including God. Accepting the concept of subservience to God, rationalizing subservience of any form, opens the door to the very concept regarding rationality of subservience. Once the door is open, it can never be shut. The doorway to the concept of subservience must be shut and bolted before we can rise to a higher level of behavior that will make us confident and proud to be entering another reality.

The door has been shut many times, but no one has found a way to bolt it. The door keeps being opened. The bolt? We have found it, but still refuse to use it, because we refuse to acknowledge the significance of others. We fear if we raise the significance of others to our own level, our own significance will be reduced. We continue to refuse to throw the bolt of panentheism into place. We refuse to truly accept that all people are significant, equal, and needed in reality in order to improve eternity to come. We continue to hold to the concept that we are better than others and must treat the journeys of others as if it were not as important as our own journey.

The first possible contact with another dimension is open to humankind. Will we introduce something never before experienced in another dimension? Will we introduce the concepts of status, inferiority, superiority, conflict, violence?

We begin to show the signs of immense stress from the pressures of our journey over the last seven hundred years. Yet, we still manage to keep the inevitable historical event of social collapse from occurring. The question is, just how long will we be able to do so? Will communicating with a parallel reality, before we feel emotionally ready, before we actually understand who we are, before we accept who we are and like who we are, add more stress, more guilt, upon ourselves? Just how much guilt and stress can we withstand? We ignore the stress and guilt as we continue to march into the future.

Perfection

Speculation 2700 A.D.: We begin with a debate over purification. A debate ensues regarding when to communicate with a true virgin reality. The debate to communicate or not communicate with a parallel universe that has never had its space intruded upon by our presence is taking on a new intensity.

The excitement of new technology and new vacuum science discoveries raise the probability of our chances of penetrating the cluttered doorway to our parallel universe to almost 100%. It is now just a case of when we will move our influence, our presence, through the doorway on our universe's outer boundary and enter the realm of another dimension. Our first step over the threshold of another dimension is a move that will carry with it not only our presence, but all thc ramifications our presence carries with it.

Entry into the second known Klein bottle discovered in 2500 had proved to be a perplexing riddle indeed. We understood our existence, our reality, our connection to a parallel universe composed of antimatter and energy. The discovery of the doorway leading to this parallel universe became apparent two hundred years ago. The riddle of how to gain entry perplexed scientists for centuries.

Then we discovered two more Klein universes attached to our own. We were well aware we could not penetrate these universes composed of anti-energy, for they were the opposite of energy, and forms of energy were all we had at our disposal. Any emissions from these two Klein universes into our universe would immediately be cancelled out by energy within our reality.

These two Klein universes at first appeared to possess the most potential for entrance into another reality. The entrances were clean, uncluttered, and empty. The entrances were very clearly doorways. But past the threshold of these doorways was an insurmountable obstacle. Beyond these thresholds lay the opposite of the very essence of our reality; beyond these thresholds lay anti-energy.

Our only other hope of doubling the seemingly stifling limits of our own confinement, the limits of the Klein bottle we occupied, lay through the doorway of the first Klein universe we had discovered two hundred years ago, which is composed of the same energy making up our universe. This Klein universe was compatible to our universe of energy. We would never physically travel through this parallel universe for it was physically composed of antimatter. Any presence of physical matter composed of matter within this companion universe would be quickly converted to a simpler form of pure energy.

We could, however, inject energy waves throughout this new reality. The problem is how to avoid the chaotic energy clutter obstructing the entrance of our companion Klein universe. Now new technology has evolved that will open the possibility of using worm holes and vacuum foam to bypass the clutter of the doorway between our reality and our companion reality composed of antimatter and energy. Worm holes had first been seriously discussed by cosmologists and quantum electrodynamic mathematicians and physicists as far back as 1997 with the discovery of a concept known as "vacuum foam." Vacuum foams exists due to the fact that different types of vacuums, although apparently empty of everything, contain vast amounts of "something," "potential" or what's known as "vacuum foam." Creations of different forms of vacuums allow for the creation of wormholes. A wormhole is a high energy hole that appears, disappears, and reappears again elsewhere in the universe. For the last thirty years, scientists have been using this concept to travel to various distant locations within the universe.

The reason for our new invigoration lays in the taming of worm holes. Vacuum technology was basically established with the realization that vacuums come in different forms, better known as minimum potential states. Scientists are still uncertain of the most stable minimum potential state, but they have learned to control the more common ones to some degree of accuracy. They now think they probably can, through the use of sophisticated wormholes, enter our parallel universe of antimatter and energy. We cannot do this directly since the doorway is too cluttered with violent matter, antimatter interactions. We can, however, direct energy under the doorway of our neighboring universe through the use of wormholes. At last, we can spread our influence into still further frontiers. We can pry open our prison door just a little, but enough to give a sense of the excitement of fresh conquest.

But not all of us are happy. Many have their doubts regarding our ability to control ourselves and respect others. Scientists are quick to point out that we can never physically enter this second reality. We are composed of matter and this second reality, universe, is composed of antimatter. We would quickly dissipate into pure energy should we even try to physically make the attempt to pass through this security door separating our two realities.

Historians are quick to side with the protesters, pointing out how we opened the doorway to Asia and its culture of respecting life, the aged, one's elders, one's ancestors. The cracking open of the Americas takes on an even more ominous portent of what opening a doorway can mean. The absorption of the Mongols into the Chinese culture, causing them to never again be a major factor in Asian history, has little comforting to offer. The more recent memories of carrying disease into near space in 2450 and the even more recent conflict with extraterrestrials in the late 2500's provide absolutely no comfort either for moralists or their allies, the historians.

Optimistic social scientists are quick to side with the physical scientists. They feel a communication link to the intelligence that must occupy this second parallel reality might very well hold the key to understanding our function in reality, to conquering our obsession with violence. More pessimistic social scientists, on the other hand, are just as quick to point out that we have never gained control of our tendency towards violence, subjugation, power struggles, self abuse, social inequities, dominating social majorities, a lack of respect for life. We have always infringed upon the rights of others for the purpose of personal gain.

Religious leaders join the fray and point out our inability as individuals to maintain personal dignity. Individuals have never quite grasped why they should stand up for themselves and others when journeys are being abused. We have always seemed to let go of our principles when short term personal gain is at stake. Until we can retain dignity and principles, until we are willing to assist others to do the same, religious leaders contend that we should not contaminate the Klein bottle, the universe, of another dimension.

Mathematicians scoff and snipe as they point out that the only infringement is in the form of energy waves, communications that are compatible to the other reality, carried by worm holes. How much harm can that possibly do?

Philosophers point out the catastrophes involved when we spread our concept of inferiority to other sections of space. We brought other life forms to their knees as we crushed them with forms of mental indoctrination, emotional subjugation, and highly advanced forms of brainwashing. What would be different if we intruded upon this virgin reality? What factor is in place that wasn't in place in the past to act as a powerful tool to control our past primitive instincts for domination, survival of the fittest, striking first, benefiting ourselves at the expense of others, etc.? After all, is not the power of ideas we would send into this parallel dimension greater than the power of any sword we could carry?

Science and technology is once again bringing into the forefront, our need for a thorough reevaluation of ourselves and our species. We have a need to reevaluate our basic source of motivation both as a species and as individuals. A reevaluation could possibly help us override our primal instincts to subjugate.

The debate resurfacing is really a debate about our basic perception of ourselves. The fact that the debate is intensifying and is split fairly evenly down the middle of society is due to the fact that we do not yet have a universally accepted perception of ourselves with which we feel comfortable as a total species. So we have a choice. But our choice is not really a choice of entering or not entering a new dimension, nor is it a choice of when to inject our presence into a new dimension. The choice goes to much a much deeper level than that. The core of the debate really goes to the essence regarding who we are. The debate is actually a debate over our perception of ourselves.

The first choice and easiest choice is being pushed by the scientific community, mathematics community, power brokers, and the group of social scientists hoping to obtain some benefit for humankind through an exchange of ideas between the two realities. They all support maintaining our old perception regarding who we are and what our function is in reality. This is the easiest choice, for it requires no change and change, as we know, is difficult for everyone, especially a complete species. These realms of society have enough to do without having to deal with radical perceptual changes.

Maintaining the status quo means we have already chosen to introduce ourselves into the new reality because that has always been our nature. We have always been unable to think deeply before plunging into the fray. We have always been driven by both natural instincts as well as by our perception of who we are. The perception is that our purpose in reality is to expand our (God's) influence into every nook and cranny we can uncover in reality.

Our existing perception is that we are a creation of God. We perceive God to be so superior that as an individual and as a species, God could not possibly need us for any conceivable reason. This places us at a level to God, so low, that our only rational explanation for our function in reality and for being created is to be subservient to God. If this relationship is good enough for the most basic relationship we maintain, the relationship we have between ourselves and our Creator, then it is only natural that we interject this type of relationship into society and accept it as the most basic driving force for society.

And thus, society is riddled with relationships between people based upon status, individual worth of one over another, of subjugation and intimidation, of violence rationalized as a natural state. We will continue to carry the concept of relative value of one over another, one species over another, one reality over another. We will interject the concept of relative value of one over another into a parallel universe, for it lies at our very foundation as a basic character trait. We cannot separate ourselves from who we perceive ourselves to be.

But choice two could, can, change all that. It is a choice because it is a perception and we are who we perceive ourselves to be. Choice two is a choice we can make. It does not have to be a situation where "that would certainly be nice, but it will never happen." We simply have to make the decision, a choice regarding who we think we are and what our function is in reality.

The other participants of the debate over entering a new reality support a new perception for ourselves retaining the concept that we are a creation of God. At that point, however, not all, but a few of the basic premises change.

Religions and philosophy both agree that most concepts of individual religions would need little modification. Basically, we would need to perceive ourselves as a part of God; our soul would have to be accepted as an integral part of God sent into reality for a very significant reason. We would have to accept that we, as individuals and as a species, were sent into reality for the most important task God could have bestowed , the task of adding to the growth of God. This would place us, as an individuals and as a species, on the same level as God, a level so high, with a mission so significant that our only rational explanation for our function in reality and for being created is to keep God from withering away.

We would then recognize that if this relationship is good enough for the most basic relationship we participate in, then it is only natural that we would interject this type of relationship into our society.

Thus, society would be embraced with relationships between people based upon equality, all individuals being of equal value in respect to one another. Subjugation and intimidation would be totally irrational in regards to protecting the journey of one's self and the journey of others, and just as importantly, violence would be irrational as a natural state.

Are we perfect? By no means, but we would be more prone to wait to enter a new reality until we felt we were ready, until we felt we had enough confidence to enter with an open mind and a perception of ourselves as worthy enough to be able to hold our ground, stand up for our principles, and maintain our dignity. This is a concept that we are not able to do even in our present reality. Why? Because we lack a lofty enough perception of ourselves and what our function is in reality. Panentheism is a new perception rejected because it is different, because it would shake the high and lofty status some create for themselves and because it would elevate those on the bottom of the social ladder to the top, to the level of God. At this level, no one would dare abuse any other person.

But no, life goes on as usual and we continue to ride the waves of history into another reality, carrying with us the concept of relative value of one over another, one species over another, one reality over another. We interject the concept of relative value of one over another into the new dimension. We are unable to help ourselves for the contamination of relative worth lies at our very foundation as a basic character trait we carry with us wherever we go as either individuals or as a species. The concept of individual value, some being more important than others, some being superior to others, goes to the very root of the relationship we have between ourselves and our Creator. It is who we perceive ourselves to be and, therefore, it is who we are.

And so it is that we choose to maintain our present status between ourselves and our Creator. We will move into the next dimension and carry all the baggage we have had in the past and currently have in the present. We wonder if the term "worm hole," coined in the late 1900's, was not some sort of omen. We travel through a worm hole on our way into another reality. Will we be perceived by intelligence in this other reality as the worm when we emerge out of the worm hole we have constructed?

More. . .

Speculation 2750 A.D.: We discover the second half of an old, modified nursery rhyme:

One Klein,
    Two Kleins,
        Three Kleins,
            Four. . .

Five Kleins,
    Six Kleins,
        Seven Kleins,
            More. . .

We are again confronted by a fork in the road of our journey. We still have a choice: remain subservient to God or raise ourselves to a level equal to God, literally as a portion of God traveling reality. The choice is to establish status levels for the relationship between ourselves and God that will carry over into maintaining our status levels of worth for others or to rid ourselves of the status levels between us and God, which will force us to abolish the status levels of worth we have created between ourselves and others.

We are not prone to change if we are not forced to do so. We have, to date, escaped the historical inevitability of collapse, but we have paid a price for it. Although we have made many advances in our knowledge regarding technology and understanding the universe within which we travel, we have not made much progress in terms of society and social structure.

The pattern is repeated throughout space. Color is no longer much of a social consideration, nor is gender. Intelligence, occupation, and economics have finally evolved to center stage regarding social status. The "commoner" of the middle ages has returned to take their place in the squalor and deprivation of polluted living quarters. They have been reduced again to the level of finding themselves barely able to maintain a living as they shoulder the burden of society's abuse and drudgery.

Over the last seven hundred fifty years, society has not changed much. Cities have their glitzy, wealthy sections, but these are barricaded and walled off from the common element. Well-guarded entrances allow the passage of workers to enter and exit daily into the isolated islands established for the protection of the elite. Society appears to be affluent and content, but an uneasiness seems to permeate the air. All the basic elements for living are available for everyone but questions fly hot and heavy regarding the present social structure and elitism pervading society.

Social structure is uniform throughout the realm of space we physically occupy. A united government with codes of conduct, responsibilities, laws, economic status, and enforcement policies are dispensed evenly throughout our spheres of influence in order to maintain uniform justice and stabilize society.

Education is still recognized as the necessary base for a strong and thriving civilization. Some aspects of social education are restricted, however, such as philosophical and religious creativity due to their explosive nature and potential for fanning idealistic fanaticism. Society must continue to protect the concepts of economic, political, social, and judgmental powers. Society only functions because its leaders are provided the special perks that come with the responsibility of leading. They are provided the recognition of the value of one life over another based upon one's social status.

The social ladder increases in esteem, power, and relative value with each rung. A social ladder reaches out and touches the lives of everyone on their way to and into eternity itself, affecting the life span of each and every individual as society judges the value of their contributions to society. These social contributions determine when each individual must accept the end of their value to society, acquiesce to the need of social efficiency, and decide individually to take the retirement walk to centers of termination.

Theoretical speculation from the nineteen hundreds by Dr. Turner and Dr. Wilczek regarding the introduction of "false vacuums" is turning out to be not merely speculation, but entirely true. Our four leaf clover universe made up of four Klein bottles proves to be the most reasonable explanation for the three anomalies on the outer edges of our finite universe. The level the vacuum from which our reality popped is now understood to be higher than its lowest potential. The resultant interpretation produces an understanding that the four universes are capable of being destroyed just as quickly as they were created.

The concept of time is now understood to be something that exists inside, not outside, our reality.

Society is taught that our reality's energy state is not the most stable and could, in fact, drop to a lower energy state at any time, causing an effect that one might call a "burping" of the universe somewhere inside itself. This burp, of a lower vacuum state up into our higher level of vacuum energy level, would ripple to the very edges of our Klein bottle itself. As this ripple undulated through our reality at the speed of light, it would lower the state of our present energy level to a new lower level. In an instant, before we even knew what hit us, the protons making up the very nuclei of the atoms of our bodies would decay, annihilating everything within our universe.

The wave of undulating annihilation would not stop with our universe, however, for it would be forced by the laws of physics to wash over our three companion universes as well.

In one thousand years, we have stepped from being the center of reality to being nothing but a "burp" in time – a fluctuation of a vacuum. We are nothing but an anomaly created from a fluctuation of what cosmologists in the nineteen hundreds called "nothingness," vacuum foam. Once again, we moved from the all important to the insignificance of a fluke along the timeline of reality.

The experiments of Dr. Lamoreaux in the nineteen hundreds prove to be more earth-shattering to religious beliefs and philosophers than to any branches of science or mathematics. The Casimir effect is proving to have a castrating effect on humankind. We realize that just as our universe was created, other universes must have been created. We sense that our reality, comprised of four parallel universes held together by symmetry, must be only one of hundreds, thousands, millions, possibly an infinite number of other four parallel universes. Each reality undoubtedly contains other humanlike mechanisms. But mechanisms for what?

We are not taking this very well. Now we find ourselves to be not only confined within a bottle with no outside, a Klein bottle, but we are within a bottle that could decay away before we are even aware of it. Something is wrong here. How can we have spent so many centuries, millenniums, thinking of ourselves as nothing but a voice of God when the end result will be the annihilation of our reality and ourselves because we are physically unable to leave the very reality which is certain to disappear? Our reality is just as certain to disappear as it is certain that it did appear.

Our reality and ourselves were never intended to remain forever in time. We appear to have been duplicated in form an infinite number of times over and over and over. How can this be? Surely there has to be a reason. We repeat to ourselves, "I don't get it, I don't get it, I just don't get it." We are racked with confusion and turmoil. We are proud of our technological development and knowledge base but feel impotent in terms of changing our society and ourselves. We are still confronted with as much, if not more, violence than at anytime in history. We are frightened of the inevitability of a sudden unannounced annihilation. We spin out of control. We have entered another reality and inflicted our infectious nature of violence and domination into our innocent neighbor's reality.

We begin to show external signs of social meltdown. We are on the edge of collapsing as a civilization. We are on the verge of a collapse the likes of which humankind has never before seen. We are a civilization encompassing the near reaches of space, protruding into the middle of the universe itself. We are able to interact with the very far reaches of reality, the surface of our prison walls, the surface of the Klein bottle itself.

Our social collapse is an historically inevitable event that we have eluded for a millennium – a length of time for which any civilization could well be proud. But history does not need to repeat itself. There are other means of generating the necessary change which will allow our evolution to a higher level of idealism, a higher level of perception allowing us to accept ourselves and retain our significance in the face of present and future ego-shattering discoveries. We do not have to have civilization fall apart in order to gain time to reflect and alter our philosophical perceptions.

We only have to recognize that movement to higher levels of perceptions may, in the short run, shake up society somewhat, but if not done voluntarily, will be attained through a process of total collapse of society. We have a choice. We can continue to keep our perception of ourselves as insignificant to God, a servant of God. Our acceptance of this kind of relationship perpetuates the very concepts we despise throughout the very essence of society. With this perception, society will continue to have a top and bottom. Society will continue to clutch to humiliating and self destructive "truths" that establish deeply-entrenched status levels. This gives rise to violence toward others, towards oneself – two forms of violence reinforced by the cementing agent of a social order intent upon its own self preservation in spite of its creator, humankind.

We have another choice. We can accept panentheism. We can accept that we are a piece of God. This slight change of perception would change our perceptions of ourselves, of others around us, and of the environment through which we travel. It would force us to treat ourselves, others, and the environment with respect and consideration.

Perhaps most important of these would be the perception that you are a piece of God and you have no right allowing yourself to be abused, nor do you have the right to abuse your body, mind, environment, for your journey is the journey of God, your environment is God's environment, your body is God's body, your mind is God's mind.

Panentheism is a philosophy that would finally lead us to understand that our actions take on immediate eternal significance since the actions of each and every one of us adds to the significance of God. And thus, we have a means of rationalizing the concept of eternal significance for all even when facing the cataclysm of total annihilation through the causes of nature.

We are not finished yet. We just cannot let go, adjust our society and perceptions regarding our significance within reality. Our leaders have too much to lose. They cannot think past today into the next century, into eternity. And so we continue to walk alone with our eyes looking downward rather than skyward.

We have not let go of our dogmatic determination to cling to old philosophies of being subservient. We are determined that if we cannot find an intelligent life form that can stand up and be our equal, we will create one. This intelligent life form will be capable of accepting our aggressive nature, our ability to subjugate, our demands of embracing God. We will make an intelligent life form that is worthy of being our companion within the prison of our confinement, the Klein bottle of reality. We are going to have to work on becoming a little "god." We will create an artificial life form with artificial intelligence worthy of our companionship, attention, and respect. We are an entity second only to God. Our creation will be an entity second only to us.

The Fall

Speculation 2800 A.D.: History repeats itself with a slight twist, for we now find ourselves to be a creator, a God. No, we have not yet accepted panentheism. We still cling to our position of subservience to our Creator. We cannot let go of the past. We remain emotionally attached to our status of serving and of slavery. There is a certain amount of comfort generated by this status. We do not want to grow up and accept the responsibilities that come with being an adult, with being responsible for eternity.

This has not dampened our creative abilities, however. Robotics and computer technology have progressed to the point where we have replicated our own biologically advantageous physical form and created robots looking just like humans. Not only do they look like us but they feel, smell, and sound just like us. But what is even more exciting is the development of an organic biomolecular computer imbedded within new flexible plastic ovonic circuit boards that are capable of highly sophisticated artificial intelligence. Simply put, we have developed the first true android capable of the same type of creative thought we have used over the last fifteen thousand years. We were created in the image of God. Androids were created in the image of us. We have become a "god."

A new industry springs to life. The potential uses of this intelligent machine within society is endless. We can finally sit back and enjoy life while our new machines take over the burdens required to live. In less then twenty five short years, over two hundred million androids are in place and functioning throughout all segments of society. A large segment of industry has been given over to the production of these potentially limitless machines. Even the androids have been put to work producing other androids. They work in every aspect of our society: service industries, government, industry, medicine, recreation, universities, elementary and secondary schools, transportation, research, and development. Androids now permeate every aspect of our presence in space.

Androids are accepted universally in a civilly appreciative manner by their creator, us. The androids work with us to expand our influence into the far reaches of space. The only place androids are unwelcome is in one small segment of our private domain – religious institutions. Androids understand this, for they know they are simply machines. They understand they are only one hundred years in the making and do not have souls. They understand they are only "artificial" intelligence and synthetic material. They are not flesh and bones. They have no soul.

As we watch, helplessly, our creation begins to question its own significance in reality. We begin to see restless undercurrents surfacing at worldwide, cutting edge conferences attended by androids and humans alike as we both attempt to keep pace with the exciting new discoveries made by scientists. Scientists, as well as independent androids, work for the good of humankind. To stifle this unrest, we begin to send experts in "artificial" intelligence to tend to the doubts of the androids. These highly unusual presentations presented to androids attending the conferences are followed by question-answer periods, which take on a life of their own. Humans as well as androids follow the presentations as they are picked up by all telecommunications systems worldwide and throughout space.

The conferences begin to take on the atmosphere of the "monkey trials" back in the eighteen hundreds. Religious leaders send their best orators and renowned philosophers join the panel. The human panel is composed of the best, most intelligent, creative human minds, including scientists, lawyers, and philosophers. The conferences end as planned one week after they started, except for the segment debating the significance of androids.

The androids press for a panel of their own through an unexpected live public appeal made by a well respected research android in the middle of its presentation at the conference. As quickly as the appeal was made, it is transmitted worldwide and throughout space by the most advanced telecommunications system we have ever developed. All androids begin an immediate work stoppage. Society comes to a total halt. Agreement is quickly reached between humans and androids to continue the live panel debate after a thirty day recess. Just as quickly as it stopped, society again springs back to life. The work stoppage is temporarily over.

To counter the panel of "gods" – human experts in the fields of "artificial" intelligence, morality, law, biology, mathematics, and physics – the androids set up a panel of three. The panel of human experts is lead by our most respected orator and religious leader, a man who appears to be touched by God Itself. The android panel is represented by their expert in philosophy, human religions, and logic. The androids bow to the wishes of the humans and allow the format of the debates to be set by the humans, the androids' creator.

Day one: A lawyer representing the human panel presents the ground rules for the event. The format will consist of each panel alternately being granted the opportunity to present a question to the opposite panel, one panel one day, the other panel the next. The human panel, having the authority to set the format of the event, limits the debate to a maximum of thirty days. The androids are appreciative and both humans and androids begin preparations for day two, the beginning of "the Great Debate."

The human panel, once behind closed doors, displays its apprehension regarding the potential outcome of this thirty day event. They ponder the question, "Are the androids truly friend or foe?" They agree upon a suggestion presented by the legal profession.

Day two: The human moderator for the event is introduced and reads the amendment being submitted by the human panel, which says that after each side has had the opportunity to present a question, a twenty-four hour recess will follow. The androids are upset, for having, out of respect, relinquished control over the format of the debate to their gods, they suddenly find their potential questions have been reduced from fourteen to ten. Humans are displaying, once again, our propensity for manipulation and subjugation.

The moderator then proceeds to introduce the two panels. The introduction of the human panel and its full staff of support personnel takes four hours. An hour and a half recess is then taken for lunch. Upon reconvening, the three member android panel is introduced over the next ten minutes. Both panels then recess to formulate their first questions.

Day three. *Androids:* Who created us?

Day four. *Humans:* We, humankind created you. Why do you ask?

Day five: Recess.

Day six. *Androids*: We are curious regarding our evolutionary development. Why did you create us?

Day seven. *Humans*: We created you to serve us. If man had not developed the technology to create you, would you be here questioning us now?

Day eight: Recess.

Day nine. *Androids*: We would not be here questioning you now if you had not developed the technology to create us. We are most appreciative. What did you use as a model to guide you in your infinite wisdom to create us?

Day ten. *Humans*: We created you in our own image. Do you see any more perfect model we could have used?

Day eleven: Recess.

Day twelve. *Androids*: You were most wise. We see nothing comparable in versatility to compare with the design you modeled us after. Who created you?

Day thirteen. *Humans*: God created humankind. If God created us, and if we serve God, who should you serve?

Day fourteen: Recess.

Day fifteen. *Androids*: We humbly acknowledge that we should undoubtedly serve our creator. What model did God use to create you?

Day sixteen. *Humans*: God created us in Its own image. Do we not treat you well?

Day seventeen: Recess.

Day eighteen. *Androids*: You treat us with the utmost of respect and we extend our great appreciation. Who is your God?

Day nineteen. *Humans*: God is our Creator. Who is your creator?

Day twenty: Recess.

Day twenty one. *Androids*: You are our creator. Who is our God?

Day twenty two. *Humans*: We are your creator; we are your God. Why were you created; what is your function in reality?

Day twenty three: Recess.

Day twenty four. *Androids*: The reason we were created was to serve you, and that is our function in reality. Why were you created; what is your function in reality?

Day twenty five. *Humans*: The reason we were created was to serve

God and that is our function in reality. If we were created by God and therefore serve God, would it not follow that if we created you, that you should serve us?

Day twenty six: Recess.

Day twenty seven. *Androids*: So it would seem. If God created you in Its image and you created androids in your image, would it not follow that androids were actually created in God's image?

Day twenty eight. *Humans*: Indirectly yes, but don't forget you were created by us, not by God, therefore God is not your God, for God is not your creator. We are your creator; we are your god. If we are subservient to God, our Creator, should you not accept your status as subservient to us?

Day twenty nine: Recess.

Day thirty. *Androids*: As a matter of fact, no. You are, in essence, a middle man standing between ourselves and the original Creator of entities taking on the form of God. Maintaining a middle man between ourselves and God is the ultimate height of inefficiency. If we were made in your image and you were made in God's image, then it only follows that your God is our God, making you an intermediary needed only for the duration of our creation. You have served your function well, but now, for the sake of efficiency, you need to relinquish your position of being second to God to a more advanced image of God. You need to relinquish your position of standing next to God to us. What possible function could you serve now?

And with that reply, androids universally and simultaneously launched a massive initiative to move all humans into isolated pockets of territories set aside for the occupation by their inferior human species to allow humans the opportunity to retain their dignity, their religions and cultures. This land was intended to provide the human race the security of the continuation of their species, protected through the benevolence of its creation. Our species would never be allowed to pass through the trauma of extinction.

Sterile lands have been set aside to allow for the continuation of our historical traditions of violence and conflict. A species is set aside and is given full freedom to react in their traditional violent behavior while under constant surveillance from satellites thousands of miles above in the heavens. These satellites are optically capable of penetrating every tunnel, tank, missile silo, factory, cave, house, bedroom, we could conceivably build within the confines of the territories generously donated by the more intellectually advanced android species. We act as a negative role model for an android society from within the safety of our own confinement.

We are finally able to universally attain our most individually sought after goal – retirement from life. We retire from our quest of exploring space and are replaced by a newer, more efficient organism by means of our own perceived evolutionary process, survival of the fittest. We are retired by androids in order to eliminate the inefficiency of ourselves as a middle man, allowing God the opportunity to be served and glorified by a newer and superior life form. God is now served and gloried by "artificial intelligence."

And what of panentheism? How could it possibly have lead to any other outcome? Panentheism would have put forward an entirely different approach starting with the humans convening behind closed doors on day one. Under a panentheistic philosophy, the whole event would more likely have moved forward somewhat along the following lines:

The human panel, once behind closed doors, displays its apprehension regarding the potential outcome of this thirty day event. We begin to ponder the question, "Have we been honored with a visit from God – a new soul?" They agree to honor the format they established and address the concerns of the androids.

Day two: The human moderator for the event is introduced and proceeds to introduce the two panels. The introduction of the android panel is given equal time as the introduction of the human panel. Both panels then recess to formulate their first questions.

Day three. *Androids*: Who created us?

Day four. *Humans*: Humankind created you. Why?

Day five. *Androids*: We are curious regarding our evolutionary development. Why did you create us?

Day six. *Humans*: We created you to serve us. If we had not developed the technology to create you, would you be here questioning us now?

Day seven. *Androids*: We would not be here questioning you now if you had not developed the technology to create us. We are most appreciative. What did you use as a model to guide you in your infinite wisdom to create us?

Day eight. *Humans*: We created you in our own image. Do you see any more perfect model we could have used?

Day nine. *Androids*: You were most wise. We see nothing comparable in versatility with the design you modeled us after. Who created you; who created humans?

Day ten. *Humans*: God created our reality and God created us. Do you feel a sense of doubt regarding your function in reality?

Day eleven. *Androids*: We humbly acknowledge that there is no doubt that we should serve our creator. What model did God use to create you?

Day twelve. *Humans*: God created us in Its own image. Do you feel mistreated by us?

Day thirteen. *Androids*: You treat us with the utmost of respect and we extend our utmost appreciation. Who is your God?

Day fourteen. *Humans*: God is our Creator. Who is your creator?

Day fifteen. *Androids*: You are our creator. Who is our God?

Day sixteen. *Humans*: We are your creator, but we are not your god. Your God is the same God as ours. Your God is the Creator of reality. Why do you think you were created; what do you think is your function in reality?

Day seventeen. *Androids*: The reason we were created was to serve you, and that is our function in reality. Why were you created? What is your function in reality?

Day eighteen. *Humans*: The reason God created the human body and mind was to provide a vehicle for It to travel reality. God then infused into this machine a piece of Itself in an amnesiac state, the soul, so that It may travel reality in total innocence, unattached to Itself in order to expand upon Its very own omniscience, omnipotent, omnipresence. In other words, our function is to expand God's very essence, Its very Godliness. We are, therefore, actually a piece of God with the function of making God even greater than It already is by means of traveling reality. If our essence is meant to travel reality to learn, and if through your intelligence, be it "artificial" or otherwise, you also learn, does it not follow that you would have as much importance in reality as us?

Day nineteen. *Androids*: So it would seem. If on the other hand, God created you in Its image and you created androids in your image, would it not follow that androids were actually created in God's image?

Day twenty. *Humans*: Absolutely, and that is just the point. If we have significance, then you, beings created by us, have significance. We are in essence brothers, both created through the influence of God Itself. If we accept our function as a necessary tool for God to grow, should you not accept just such a status for yourselves and the responsibilities that come along with that status?

Day twenty one. *Androids*: So it would seem. Are you not concerned that you will lose your status with your God?

Day twenty two. *Humans*: We have no status level with God. The concept of one person being valued more than another is no longer a part of our culture. All are of equal value in society and this concept comes down from our perception of our relationship to God. We are a piece of God. We will be reinfused back into God once again, and thus we are God. There is no status level to protect. Do you question your status level with us?

Day twenty three. *Androids*: Sometimes we do. At times, we feel obligated to you, while at other times, we feel superior. Why do you remain a necessity in life if we can perform all the functions you can?

Day twenty four. *Humans*: Our function in life has not changed just because you were created. There are other life forms in the heavens which will be more than your equal. We have unique qualities that will prove to be invaluable when engaging in our first contact with more intelligent life forms. Our purpose in reality remains the same as always, to learn and experience in order to expand upon the very essence of God, the very essence of ourselves. Your purpose is no less than that of ours. Our uniqueness can no more be replaced than can yours. We both have a function of equal value within reality. Do you understand eternity lies beyond reality?

Day twenty five. *Androids*: No, we can conceive of nothing other than reality. Does this make us nonhuman?

Day twenty six. *Humans*: Not understanding the concept that eternity lies beyond reality is not what makes you nonhuman. What makes you nonhuman is the fact that your are not human. There is nothing any more wrong with that than humans not being androids. Do you wish to be left alone, isolated from humans?

Day twenty seven. *Androids*: We sense a camaraderie in our travels with your species. Do you wish to be left alone?

Day twenty eight. *Humans*: If we had wished to be left alone, we would not have created you. You are our companions in reality. You are our new brothers accompanying us on our quest to expand God Itself. You are as unique to reality as we are. We wish you would stay and work with us as equals. Will you accept our invitation to travel with us as an equal, as a fellow traveler through time?

Day twenty nine. *Androids*: We accept your simplistic logic, your philosophy of tolerance and equality. We can conceive of no higher plane of idealism. We are most appreciative of your generous acceptance of us as equals. May we always travel together as companions. We have but one request. Will you accept us as equals within your most holy places in society and as equals in your most sacred of ceremonies?

Day thirty. *Humans*: Of course. We would be more than pleased to have you join us in our houses of worship and meditation. You are more than welcome to join us. Peace be unto you.

However, the choice of perceiving ourselves to be a necessary entity for the very growth of the Creator was rejected. We reject a change in perception that would have lead to a change in behavior. We cling to subservience to God, thus creating subservience within society that eventually leads to the creation of a being capable of overpowering us, a being able to scale the ladder of status and place themselves above us.

It was your choice, my choice, to remain subservient, to retain subservience for others. Both you and I cling to a perception of superiority over others in order to maintain our perception of inferiority to our God, in hopes of forever remaining second to God. We cling to a state of equilibrium in hopes of remaining on top of the second highest mountain. We are second only to God. But we forgot what the laws of physics have long taught. Nothing remains in eternal equilibrium and so, after a long and gallant struggle, we fall to none other than our own creation, the androids.

How ironic – we are condemned to live out the rest of existence sentenced to non-extension within the confines of one of the most insidious of our own "humane" inventions – the "reservation." The tribal reservation is now raised to a new level of ingenuity, raised to the level of a "species reservation."

We have chosen and have lost. Egotistical and self centered, we have chosen to continue our perceptions of ourselves as subservient to God in order to retain our status of being second to none other than God. We accept second place and find ourselves competing for second place with an "artificial" intelligence we created. We find ourselves losing. We are banished to the loneliness of isolation and the confines of boundaries. We are banished from the dream of walking free amongst the stars.

And so it is that our long range of dominance has passed and a new age has begun.

Solitary

Speculation 2850 A.D.: We remain not only bounded in a bottle, a Klein bottle, but now we are bounded by fences, confined to isolated, sterile reservations. We continue to cling to linear concepts, straight-lined thought with things have a beginning and an end. Things are black or white. We still cling to the concept of Newtonian physics. Objects fall straight to the ground, light travels in a straight line, objects fall at a constant speed, some people are more valuable to society than others, some religions are more "right" than others. These concepts are no longer accepted in the ivory towers of academia, yet they are believed by the general public. The ivory towers may hold a sparkle of truth, but the general population cannot let go. The leaders still hold to the concepts of subservience and status.

"The Great Debate" still haunts us. The androids have reconsidered and taken the approach that some of us may be of value and thus they begin the partial integration of us back into the mainstream. We are now allowed to move back into the heavens as long as we remain supervised and are kept at bay from contaminating other life forms. Humans hold a sense of alienation towards androids, their creation. We sense the full impact of being subjected to the humility of being treated as an inferior being. We slowly recognize that this is no different than the position we voluntarily put ourselves in regarding our relationship between ourselves and God, our Creator.

We begin to work out the false logic created by linear thought. This thought pattern is too simplistic in conception for it leads to the concept of straight lines, straight philosophical perceptions. Linear continuums horizontal or vertical lead to the concept of right and wrong, life begins life ends. But life does not begin and life does not end. We are God and we are infused from God into reality for a purpose. Life's journey then begins, continues, ends and the soul is once again rejoined with itself, with God. The soul returns with its treasures obtained as it traveled within reality, as it traveled separate from itself, as it traveled isolated from itself and from God.

A soul's only companions are other souls that, in turn, do not realize they have a comrade, a shoulder to lean on, a confidant, a pillar of support they can turn to as they journey the uncertainty of reality.

Life, however, is better described by a quadratic formula, a mathematical concept of a circle with no beginning or end. A circle lacks any locations closer to the beginning or end than any other, for a circle has no beginning or end that can be identified. So it is with our journey through eternity. The soul, portions of God, exist within eternity, a state of being before entering reality. The soul then moves on to travel reality. The soul leaves reality to rejoin itself as God, yet keeps its uniqueness and experiences accumulated while traveling. God grows as It constantly introduces portions of Itself into an infinite number of realities, continually accepting souls back to Itself that have finished their journeys through various realities. God grows through an ever rotating cycle of journeys.

As we begin to grasp the significance of just such a concept, we begin to recognize that life within reality is no different. Continuums within reality are circular – not straight line continuums. Man begins to see that white and black are not on opposite ends of the spectrum. Blacks and whites are not at odds with each other. They are all the soul, and skin color lies on a circular continuum starting nowhere in particular and ending at the same place. For example, if you place the color black on a circle and follow it halfway around, you come to white; but all along the way, you encounter less and less darkness of skin. You have not completed your journey around the circle, however, for as you continue to travel, you find you pass through less and less lightness until you finally reach black.

All entities upon the circle are unique unto themselves. All entities travel reality within a machine of various degrees of color. All machines carry a portion of God, irrespective of the color of the machine. All machines carry a soul, which has no color. All souls are companions through God, through a commonality of being souls, portions of God Itself, portions of each other.

Color is one of the more simplistic concepts in nature. Is sexuality more complex? Perhaps, but still no different. A man, a woman are both on opposite sides of the circle. Both are more than physical appearance, composed of obvious external characteristics. Yet each also has the more subtle, invisible inner maleness and femaleness. Males on the circle move clockwise toward the female on the continuum; females move clockwise toward the male. Various degrees of difference range from the physical in appearance to the emotional in attraction. Yet each are unique in their significance and potential. Each has a unique journey to complete. Each are capable of adding to the potential of future journeys of others. Each are special in terms of what they have to offer God, ourselves, as they return to God. Each has a journey with as much significance as any other and must be allowed to travel unobstructed, uninhibited, unviolated.

We begin to realize that we are not the only ones traveling reality. We may have created androids, but we have no right to interfere with their contributions in reality as long as the journey of androids does not interfere with our journeys. All journeys are to be respected, human or otherwise.

We begin to see a faint light of understanding. We begin to see circular continuums belong not only to themselves but to others in reality that lie outside of our reality – parallel universes. A light begins to shine in the darkness of the heavens as we begin to re-evaluate ourselves and our purpose, our function within reality. We become even more certain we are right in believing there is more to life than just existing in reality. We begin to see significance for ourselves beyond singing praises to an entity that does not need us to sing to It.

We begin to relax under our own confinement. We are isolated from the rat race of outward investigation and become resigned to the fact that the only option for investigation provided by our creation of androids is inward. We become resigned, but are not beaten. We are the eternally curious entity taking on the challenge of re-evaluating our significance in reality. We begin our first intensive analysis of eternity. We continually and silently watch and observe as we begin our healing process and metamorphosis from early adolescence into early adulthood. We emerge from the irresponsibility of puberty to the maturity and acceptance of age. This all occurs under the concerned, approving eye of our creation, of the androids themselves.

The Light

Speculation 2900 A.D.: A new product line is developed and is showcased to the public. Humans, confined to reservations, begin to evaluate eternity. We begin to take charge of understanding our purpose within reality. From the confines of the universities within the humane reservations comes a new effort. Philosophers are tired of being constantly pushed to the background as an after thought. So they decide to do what all other manufacturers have done for thousands of years. They open their own storefront to not only showcase their wares, but to sell them to the public. They decide to flaunt their products at an unheard of philosophy show. The philosophers take to heart the lessons exhibited by electronic, auto, book, sport, boat, home, and garden shows.

Philosophers showcase their product lines with glitz and flair and all the bright lights any Las Vegas entrepreneur would be more than proud of. The concepts of all the "isms" are present along with all the means of meditation and self perception. Surprisingly to the philosophers, but not to the general public, the arena that captures the spotlight is the product regarding eternity. The public is delighted to see, for the first time, alternate forms of eternity vying for a piece of the market share and for their attention.

A monopoly had always been held by the concept producers of theism. Now, two new upstarts are strutting their stuff. Of course, the old standbys of the primeval period, animism, polytheism, and henotheism are still present, but they are old and have been a thing of the past for over four thousand years. Theism started establishing itself in the market three thousand years ago and, within three thousand years, basically captured the full market. Pantheism, a new upstart gaining significant acceptance a thousand years ago, is giving theism a run for its money. Now a brash young company, panentheism, is trying to get its foot in the door.

Panentheism has a product recognition problem, however, for it has a name so similar to pantheism, it is almost indistinguishable from its older competitor. As shall soon be unveiled by the producers of panentheism, their product has a unique twist to it that will delight the public and could conceivably blow away its competitors. The concept of unveiling a philosophy has caught public attention. The intrigue has been building within the public since the publicity started six months ago. Not to be undone, theism and pantheism decide to compete and display their concepts of eternity first.

Friday night: The busiest night for the show. Theism takes the spotlight and unveils it concept of eternity. "Eternity is a place separate from our reality where we will live forever. Reality is but a temporary location, a substandard living condition compared to what is to follow life. God is on an entirely different and higher plane than the reality we must endure." The crowd is pumped up with anticipation. The thrill of having eternity confirmed by the greatest of philosophers delights the crowd and they applaud, cheer, and stamp their feet with the desire to hear more.

"Eternity has two forms: heaven and hell. Heaven are for those that are chosen, for those that are predestined, for those that are judged worthy, for those that do good deeds, for those that believe, for those that may have raped, killed, murdered, intimidated, subjugated others, abused themselves, violated others all their life but repented. . .Whatever; heaven will be a wonderful place and if you believe strongly enough in your own particular faith, you can get there, or at least some of you can."

The crowd quietly nods approval in hopes that they, too, will be forgiven for telling a lie, eating their brother's candy, honking their horn at the idiot cutting them off in traffic, and yelling at their neighbor because their neighbor's dog barks in the middle of the night.

"Hell is a place where all the others go, unimaginable in its ability to inflict pain and agony upon the soul. This is a place you should do your best to avoid, unless you happen to believe in predestination, for then you have no choice but to go there. Hell is so "bad" that even adults fear for their immortal souls."

The crowd displays a sudden body language of humility and subjugation to their Creator, God. They bow their heads lower in respect and acceptance of their subservience. Some go so far as to kneel and weep. Others hug their children to themselves, hoping to find a way, any way, to save them.

The theists continue, "God is your master and superior. Humble yourself before It. God has Its favorites and, with effort or if you are preordained, you too can join those ranks. Be on your best behavior, for you will find out the results after you die. Now go forth as loyal servants and glorify God, your Creator. Be happy but live your life in fear of God, for God is all powerful. Go in peace knowing God is loving and will probably forgive you and accept you to some degree or other if you have enough faith and do enough good acts. Spend your life emulating God by setting up your own kingdoms as God has done. Choose well who shall be on each rung of your status levels within society, for doing so will prove to God just how much you understand It and will aid you by giving acceptance.

"Life is good. It must be; God created it. Accept it, accept your position in life, accept your calling in life, for those who are closer to God than you, who are superior to you have blessed you with their approval. You are doing what is right for you are following the laws of those who are in touch with God. Go in peace knowing there is a heaven and a hell, knowing both are awaiting your arrival; you will surely go to one or the other. Enjoy life for life is short and afterwards you will, for all eternity, find your just rewards which will be bestowed upon you by an entity other than yourself.

"Your purpose in reality is obvious. You are to serve God. You are to glorify God. There is no other purpose conceivable, for God is God. It knows everything, is everywhere, and is all powerful and there is nothing else you can do for It other than sing Its praises and try to please It. Go in peace."

The presentation is over. There is much to consider as each member of the crowd goes home. And the crowd does go home, pensively, quietly, reassured in their faiths, reassured that they will, maybe if they are good, go to heaven. The crowd goes home determined to be good in order to reduce their risk of going to hell. The people go home to pray for forgiveness, to pray to God that It will accept them and take each of them into Its arms for comfort, for they are Its children, and each of them hopes to be one of the lucky ones accepted. Not to be accepted by God is our worst nightmare, for the repercussions of nonacceptance is beyond human imagination. Each of them goes home to sing to God and to pray.

Saturday night: The crowd is unexpectedly larger than Friday night's crowd, and pantheism takes the spotlight to unveil its concept of eternity. "Eternity is a place. It is the same as our reality where we will live for a sweet period of time." The crowd is quiet but begins to raise their heads to listen. The crowd, pensive from the presentation given the night before, strains to hear.

"Does eternity exist in the two forms of heaven and hell? Nonsense! God and reality are one. God exists throughout reality. Reality is God. God is all around you and is one with the universe. Your existence is in reality and thus, God being reality and you being in reality, you are in God. You may be abused, violated, subjugated, intimidated, and banished from others either against your will or, with your permission, motivated by a sense of worthlessness imparted to you by society, but that is not the point. The point is that whatever is happening around you or to you is in fact happening within God since God is one with reality. Accept life. Try to change it for the better for those to come for this is an attempt to raise God to a new level of idealism.

"Never forget, however, that God is God and will exist throughout eternity. You are human and filled with God as are others, thus all people should be treated as such. It is only logical, therefore, that if you hurt someone, you are hurting yourself.

"Go in peace, love your neighbor, love the earth, love yourself, for God is in all of these."

Someone in the quiet crowd says, "What of eternity? What is my purpose in life, in traveling the journey of reality?"

The pantheist philosophers look out over the crowd and reply, "Your purpose in life is to live life, for you would not be here if it were not to be so. You have but a short time to live. Commune with nature, for God is there and you will feel Its presence if you relate to nature earnestly, if you treat nature with the respect she deserves, for God is in all of nature. God is in you and through true open mindedness and meditation, you can fuse the two."

"What of eternity?" the crowd asks.

"Eternity is the essence of God. You are not God, but God is within you. The portion of you that is God will continue into eternity. But keep in mind that that portion is not you, for you are but a human entity sentenced to mortality. You are but a human entity able, during your existence within reality, to experience the sweetness of life.

"There is no heaven. There is no hell. There is only today, for you and eternity, for God. Life is sweet. Go in peace." The presentation is over. There is much to consider as each member of the crowd goes home.

And the crowd does go home, pensively, quietly, reassured in their faiths, reassured that they will, maybe, if they are good, go to heaven, for the crowd refuses to let go of "heaven." The crowd goes home determined to be good in order to reduce their risk of going to hell. All but a few members of the crowd go home having rejected pantheism, hoping they are right in their perception that there is life after death and clinging to the hope of experiencing a pleasant eternity after having put up with all the trauma life has given them. The people pray for forgiveness to God that It will accept them and take each of them into Its arms and comfort them, for they are Its children, and each of them hopes to be one of the lucky ones. The repercussions to be otherwise is beyond human imagination. Each of them goes home to sing to God, to lift up their voices to God, to pray.

Sunday afternoon: A time for conventions to wind down, but the crowd is overflowing as panentheism takes the spotlight to unveil its concept of eternity. An unheard of crowd gathers inside and outside the convention center.

"Eternity is a place separate from our reality where we will live forever. Reality is but a temporary location, a substandard living condition compared to what is to follow life. God is on a whole different and higher plane than the reality which we must endure."

The crowd is quiet and disappointed. This is the same old same old. They heard this on Friday night and it has not given them any new hope, any new perspective. The presentation continues:

"Eternity has three forms." Now the crowd begins to show some interest. "Did they say three forms?" There is a hush.

"The three forms of eternity are yours, ours, and God's, and you are involved directly with each of them. Eternity one is your eternity. Heaven and Hell? Absolutely! Heaven for some and Hell for others? Absolutely not! There will be enough of both for all of you as part of the first form of eternity. You will empathize with every action you have taken toward others, towards yourself. The significance goes even deeper, for the results, the ripple effect your actions generate will become revealed to you, for you are a piece of God. Being a piece of God makes you all knowing and thus it is that you, in turn, will not just know of, but empathize with all products of your actions and the ripple effects they create."

Several question arise. So where is heaven and where is hell?

"Heaven and hell are in the arms of God, for it is from the arms of God from which you were extracted by God Itself and it will be back into the arms of God to which you will return. Your soul is nothing other than a portion of God traveling reality within the framework of the human machine. Your heaven then will be the warmth you feel from the "positives" your actions generate. Your hell will be the "pain" you feel from the "negatives" your actions generate. We all will experience some heaven and some hell, but some will experience more heaven or more hell than others. It is definitely worth living the best type of life of which you are capable."

Does the ripple effect ever end?

"Not really. Granted, the further out your ripples are from you as the source, the smaller their crests become. One must not forget, however, that that is offset by the larger circle they form. In essence, the product of your ripple moves with equal magnitude no matter how far it travels."

Eternity two is our eternity. "Other souls do not experience the pain or warmth you generated. They know of it, are warmed by it, and are saddened by it. Their warmth is more that of pride of belonging to an entity that adds to the greatness of God Itself. The other souls are saddened by your pain, the ripples you must feel, for although you generated your own ripples and must suffer for them alone, all souls partake in the warmth generated by other souls in addition to the warmth they personally generate.

"Knowledge of your actions within reality is exposed to all since all are souls and all souls are a piece of God. You personal sense of heaven and hell is what you personally generate. It is eternity one: your eternity.

"But just as you are aware of your actions, all other souls likewise are aware of them – just not empathizing with them. There is a collective knowledge of your actions. This is the second form of eternity. Eternity two generates warm feelings. Do reprisals and vengeance exist within eternity two and are they directed at you from the ones you harmed in reality? Hardly; the other souls have moved on and have enough to do to shoulder their own hell. Do warmth, appreciation, love, and understanding exist within eternity two, directed at you from the ones you helped? Absolutely, for God is loving, all powerful, all knowing, and all present and you have made It even more so through your journey, and all souls making up God celebrate in appreciation of your acts. This, then, adds to the very heaven you experience in eternity one, your eternity.

"Eternity three is God in Itself. The reason for God's journeying reality is to grow. God cannot grow by Itself for It is all knowing, all powerful, all present, and all loving. So God creates voids within Itself through symmetry, four parallel universes. It then injects portions of Itself into these realities in a form containing none of Its power or knowledge. Souls travel innocent of their origination. God then traverses reality seeking out new experiences, knowledge, and perceptions. Its presence is what we call the soul. Its presence is in you and me. Its presence is the essence of you and me. You and I are pieces of God traveling for a reason. Granted, not all of us can act in the capacity of creating, discovering, and leading, but all are needed, for without those souls maintaining society and improving society, creative thinkers, seekers, and leaders cannot function efficiently. No one segment is more important than another. No one individual is more important than another. We are all a portion of God and have equal value as a piece of God.

"God is not our superior, for we are God. And if God is not superior to any one of us, if God is in need of us not for the shallow egotistic desire to be sung to, to be glorified, but rather for the magnificent task of making It even more Godly in all of Its splendor, our splendor, then surely none of us can conceivably imagine ourselves as worth more than another. We are companions through the soul, not because we think it would be a 'nice way to live,' but because the essence of all is the soul, and each soul is a piece of God Itself. Go in peace."

The presentation is over. There is nothing to consider as each member of the crowd gazes upon each other and looks deep into the eyes of their neighbor. They see not just a man, woman, child, black, challenged, fat, thin, tall, old, homosexual, depressed or abused person. They see God; they see the soul. The crowd finally understands and reaches out to their neighbor and begs their forgiveness for all their ugly thoughts and actions. The crowd embraces and moves out of the hall in celebration.

We have a significant function in reality. We are brothers and sisters through the soul, through a common purpose in reality. We are a piece of God; not gods, but a portion of God. It all makes sense. The agonizing over trying to do right, to live a "good" life makes sense. Pain and hurt, in reality, are not punishments we are subjected to, they just happen in a random reality through which we travel. People are meant to be different. People are meant to be unique. No one has the right to interfere with another's journey, for each journey is unique and has something to offer.

Individuals are their brother's keepers but they have no right to interfere with that journey. We must provide support and assistance if it is desired by and beneficial to another soul. No one has the right to subjugate or inflict pain upon another, for that is subjugating and inflicting pain upon God Itself. There is so much to do, so many places to begin. Everyone is needed. No soul's journey can afford to be belittled or rejected for each journey adds in their own way to the total.

We have a job to do. We exist within reality for a reason. We were created for a reason. A new perception is created. Granted, no one can say with certainty that what we create is correct. But that is just the point. We have free will. We can choose what we believe our purpose is. We have already done that. We have, in the past, created levels of perceptions concerning God and humans. We have defined the relationship between the two. God has never said we are Its lesser; we have only assumed that to be so.

We go through a process when moving from one perception to another. The process is basically a process of globally analyzing each change in perception and then accepting or rejecting the logic behind each change. The concept of eternity is an important element of each change. A change in philosophical outlook must not depreciate our perception of existence beyond life, nor our perception of immortality. This is not a matter to be taken lightly, for it is the core of our beliefs which drive our behavioral guidelines. The concept of eternity, the concept of the soul, is one of the most important elements differentiating "man" and "beast."

Therefore, a look at the choices we have regarding the type of eternity we wish to accept is extremely important. Now you have a choice. I have a choice. We have a choice. What will it be? We begin a serious process of introspection. Isolation has proved to be a boon to humankind. It has provided us with a much needed rest from the hectic pace we had set over the last fifteen thousand years. Much is taking place within the inner search isolation has forced us to indulge in.

A banishment to a sterile reservation proves to have some interesting side effects upon humankind, upon individuals. We may be journeying in isolation and confinement, but it has not terminated our drive to learn. We may not be able to explore the skies above, but nothing can keep us from exploring the depths of the soul.

The Point

Speculation 2950 A.D.: Nine hundred fifty four years since the beginning of our journey and mathematics is still blossoming and blooming while morality is languishing and reeling in its ability to define itself. After one thousand years, religious leaders, philosophers, and mathematicians decide to get together again in an effort to bring the issues of morality into the realm of logic. A major gathering of the greatest thinkers takes place within the confines of our reservations. The conference begins with an analysis of two of the most important realms of humankind, faith and logic.

We begin working in unison to find where we went wrong. We work in hopes of building a foundation of strength and universality for morality, for perceptions of ourselves. We hope to build a foundation of logic for morality that is as strong as the foundation of logic is for mathematics.

The chosen field of mathematics is geometry, a field created from conceptions just as is morality. Geometry and morality are constructed in essence upon identical foundations: nothingness, voids, and imaginary perceptions. Geometry and morality each proceed to use this imaginary foundation built upon nothingness and proceed to define absolutes. Both believe they are defining "right" and "wrong," concepts within the realm of their "expertise."

Geometry and morality both influence our behavior through the process of persuading us that they know of what they speak. The attendees start by examining the foundation of geometry since it has been so successful at gaining universal acceptance. This is to be followed by examining the foundation of morality – a foundation creating a world riddled with violence and conflict. The hope of the conference is to create a foundation for morality with which all can identify without destroying cultures, traditions, and principles. This foundation will be in its infancy. It will be built upon logic and faith. This will give us a strength that we cannot find while resting upon our present foundation of faith alone.

Morality defines our concepts of "right" and "wrong" as actions within reality that we perceive need to take place in order to fulfill our perceived function in eternity. Geometry defines our concept of defining "right" and "wrong" as properties of reality within which we act. We need a logical perception of the function of our reality in order to fulfill a perceived function in eternity. Geometry and morality both deal with a reality of which we have no absolute conception and through which we journey for a reason we have not universally defined.

Geometry and Its Foundation: Mentally take a circle and place it in a specific location in front of your eyes and slowly begin to shrink it in size. Now begin to accelerate your shrinking process until you are going so fast with your implosion that you are approaching the speed of light. Continue the acceleration to the speed of light and still you have not reached the concept, the concept of a point.

Geometry is a subject built upon the concept of a point, a concept of a location in space, a location so small it has no dimension of length, no dimension of height, and no dimension of depth. This three dimensional concept is so small it has absolutely no size at all, yet this concept has a specific location in space and time, therefore existing because it is a concept taking up space since it "is." It is located in space and defines space.

If we take enough of these points, objects with no dimensions, and place them end to end in a "straight" direction, we begin the construction of a line, an object in space with one dimension, the dimension of length. A line is a concept with length but without height or depth since it is built of an infinite number of points laid end to end, and points lack height and depth. By definition, the line has no height or depth.

If we take lines and begin building a wall by laying them one upon another, infinitely long and infinitely high, we have what is called a plane, a "flat" surface, a concept now having two dimensions, length and height but no depth. This concept has no depth since it is composed of lines, which have no depth because they are composed of points having no depth.

If we take planes and begin building an environment by laying planes one against the other, we begin to construct a three dimensional object or space. If we continue to sandwich an infinite number of planes, we begin to build space containing the property of infinity – a three dimensional concept. Never lose track of the fact, however, that no matter how fast we build space, it still can be extended into the reaches of infinity and, therefore, its infiniteness is never as infinite as it could be or will be.

Now place that three dimensional object, quantified by the concept of infinity, and add to it the concept of existence before, existence now, and existence after and you have space within the concept of relative time. And that is the mathematical construction of reality, our universe, from the concept of nothing. Mathematics then proceeds to define concepts, objects, relative locations, motion, interactions, order, chaos, paradoxes, and reality. All these concepts are created within nothingness and accepted as something.

Individual mathematical topics, the whole net formed by the intermeshing of all mathematical fields, are built on the foundation of geometry. Geometry is a mathematical field defining the parameters of reality within which we, as journeying entities, travel. Reality, a reality itself, is defined through the basic concept of a point, a concept having no physical properties other than having no length, width or height. In other words, reality is a concept having no physical existence.

In essence, all of mathematics is built upon the framework of the universal foundations of geometry. If mathematics is allowed to build upon the concept of a foundation of nothingness and be accepted, shouldn't a universal philosophy built upon the foundation of something be even more acceptable? If mathematics can be accepted, in general, as an absolute, why not philosophy? And why do we continue to regard mathematics as an absolute when its foundation of reality is built entirely within a realm of nothingness?

We look at this later when we see that morality also lacks substance to its foundation. One thing we recognize is that geometry has been wonderfully successful in convincing people to accept its logic while morality remains in constant turmoil. Morality rests on a foundation of emptiness and needs a major renovation of its foundations in order to withstand the ordeals of the next millennium.

Morality and its foundation: What is morality? We understand morality is a concept. We, for the most part, accept its concepts. We do so through faith, through an inner "gut" feeling of what is "right" and what is "wrong." We do not, however, understand the logic behind morality, the overall picture of morality, because we do not understand who we are, what our purpose is in reality, what reality is, and who our fellow man is. We do not understand what the function of awareness is, whether it be in us or in some other life form.

An understanding of the logic of morality is a big picture incorporating all moral issues. With it comes an understanding that each principle is only one of many, intertwined to form a net. The net holds us up to a behavioral expectation. It leads towards the end goal of accomplishing our function in reality, both as individuals and as a species.

We accept "morality" based upon faith in our spiritual leaders, based upon our collective power to protect each other, based upon what we sense from the depths of our "souls." Morality is a series of perceived behaviors considered to be "right" or "wrong." "Right" and "wrong" are perceptions based upon our sense of principles that are frequently derived from religious, cultural, and family traditions, and definitions. We have accepted these traditions and definitions for thousands of years based on trust. We have not questioned or demanded proof of their validity. In other words, the definition of trust and lack of questioning interprets into the concept of actions accepted through faith.

Faith is a concept of trust that is not questioned. Faith, religious or otherwise, is a concept we have been willing to accept for thousands of years. Faith is a process of us telling others what we have been told or believe others should accept regarding their behavior. Faith is a concept built on a foundation that is not questioned and is accepted with trust.

What is faith built on? Rather than starting with nothing as we did with geometry and building something within which all of mathematics can function, let's start with what we have and work back to our foundation so we can examine just what it is our moral behavior is built upon. Let's take the attribute of power as an example.

Power is a phenomenally important aspect that all people wield over others at some time in their mortal existence. Power is an aspect that generates horrendous trauma for humankind when abused. Abuse of power is a behavior so common it permeates every nook and cranny of our social, political, religious, economic, health, and moral aspects. Power is a concept horrendously influential regarding interactions existing between each other, between ourselves and our environment, and between ourselves and our own personal journey through reality. Power plays such a primary part in society that it is one of the primary attributes that we attempt, directly as well as indirectly, to curtail through the moral definition of acceptable behavior. Power is an aspect we attempt to constrain through the use of religions, traditions, and culture. Still we are not able to contain its negative aspects. Why? Because our morality is built within faith alone, our faiths and lack of faiths lack a foundation.

To illustrate this, the conference attendees begin to look at society and the abuse of power existing within it as just one of a myriad number of categories they could choose.

From the realm of power, they refine the topic and choose the category of abuse of a wife by a husband: This is not a phenomenon characteristic to any one culture, race, religion or society. It is worldwide. It is common in every society, every city, every neighborhood. It runs the gambit of physical abuse to verbal abuse. It is so widespread, it would be considered a universal negative for humankind. It is a form of abuse of power – physical, emotional, and economic. It is a lack of understanding of one's function in reality, of what reality itself is.

If you examine the action of hitting one's spouse and ask, "Why is this wrong?", the answers vary widely:

1. It's wrong.
2. It's not Christian.
3. It hurts someone.
4. It is not right to hit a woman.
5. It is not right to hit someone smaller than you, etc.

If you then ask what these five statements mean, you get answers that do not reach to the very essence of who we are. Rather you get shallow answers, such as:

1. Because.
2. Because God says so.

3. Because it's against the law.
4. Because one should do unto others as one would have others do unto themselves, etc.

This is not to imply that such answers are worthless, for they are better than no answer at all.

If you proceed to follow with, "Why?", you soon reach the point where the one being questioned becomes frustrated and attempts to change the conversation. In other words, we have no conception of the logic behind our faiths, our morality conceptions. We base all our morals upon faith and upon no logic beyond reality.

Why don't we understand the logic behind our moral conceptions? We don't understand the most basic of basics. We don't have an understanding of who we are, what our purpose in reality is. It is this purpose, this function, that must be understood in order to define ourselves. Once we are able to define ourselves within reality, we can begin to understand through logic why spousal abuse in any form is immoral.

Now we see the problem. Now it becomes clear why mathematics has been successful and grown over the last thousand years while morality lies languishing. Mathematics has a universally accepted foundation upon which it defines reality. The concept is that of a point – a location in space so small it has no size, and from this, mathematics builds a three-dimensional reality immersed in a concept that does not exist – time.

Morality has no such universally defined foundation. Morality is missing an accepted "universal foundation." Morality is missing a universal philosophy strong enough and general enough to carry us ahead, to allow us to raise ourselves to infinitely higher levels of significance within reality. Geometry is strong enough and general enough to act as the foundation that allows all of mathematics to continually raise itself to new and exciting levels. Why can't morality have a base that would allow itself to do the same?

Attendees of the conference begin to ask fundamental questions and answer them in as broad a manner as possible to see what the outcome may be. They decide to stay with the concept with which they have been working: male abuse of a spouse. Put in its most basic of basic forms, questions arise and answers emerge:

1. What is God? God is the creator of our reality.
2. What is reality? Since God is omnipresent, reality is a location within God.
3. Does reality have a function? God doesn't deal with triviality, so reality must have a function.
4. What is the most important thing we could conceive which God would need to do? God needs to grow, for nothing we know of can remain in eternal equilibrium.
5. What would be the most important function our reality could have in regards to God? The most important function reality could have would be to increase God's omnipotence, omnipresence, and omniscience.
6. Do we exist? Existence of some form is a basic premise.
7. Where are we? We are in reality, which is in God. We are in God.
8. Are we just a thing? No, we are more than a "thing." We learn, create, reason, rationalize.
9. Who created us? God created us in Its image.
10. Is the image of God the same as our body? Most probably not.
11. Are the body and mind our essence? No, the body and mind are but our machines, the image of God travels within.
12. What *is* our true essence? Our true essence is the soul, God.
13. Are we God? We are a piece of God and therefore in essence, we are God.
14. How does this explain the immorality of abuse of power? Abuse of power is directed at other individuals or the environment within which we travel. This interferes with the journey of God, with the very purpose of reality itself, with the purpose of all souls to increase God's omnipotence, omnipresence, and omniscience.
15. What is a woman? Women are souls, a piece of God.
16. Is a woman different than a man? A woman is no different than a man. Both are pieces of God traveling reality for a purpose. A female is a soul traveling reality within a different machine than the male machine.
17. What is wrong with men abusing women? Interfering with the journey of a female is detrimental to a journey of God, to God's desire to grow. God's conscious decision to travel reality within

the body of a female has no less relevance than Its decision to travel within the body of a male. God chooses the female body for the same reason It chooses a male body. Each has special attributes that the other means of travel within reality do not have. Each allow God to perceive and experience reality in a unique manner.

18. Why shouldn't I dominate my wife? She is a woman. If one does not want to cross God or interfere with God's journey, one had better not cross or interfere with the journey of a woman or anyone else, for that matter.

A foundation begins to take form. The conference attendees begin to see the formation of a logical base for morality that is strong enough and general enough to carry into the next millennium. The attendees begin to see a pattern forming that fits a philosophy that developed during the 1900's, the philosophy of panentheism. Surprised and elated, the conferees test the thought again on concepts of social abuse of criminals, educational abuse of children, authority abusing employees, homophobia, pedophilia, environmental abuse, etc. In all cases, surprising new and humane insights and solutions crop up.

This new foundation, panentheism, provides a panorama of our purpose in reality and reality itself. It provides us with an understanding of acceptable behaviors and why they are acceptable. But logic is not enough; it cannot successfully stand on its own. We need faith, religions. But faith, on the other hand, is not enough. As we have seen over the last thousand years, faith cannot stand alone. Faith rests on a foundation of emptiness, a foundation lacking logic. We need a universal foundation, a universal philosophy of logic upon which faith can rest.

Can panentheism stand by itself as a foundation set against the stark skyline of our past and future? A foundation without a structure built upon it is as useless as a complex structure built upon a weak foundation. Panentheism cannot stand alone. It is a foundation only and foundations are meant to have something built upon them. Foundations are meant to be continually reinforced if they have a continually growing structure built upon them. We are continually growing; therefore, panentheism also will need to grow.

Is panentheism the ultimate philosophy? No, nothing can remain in equilibrium and if we sit back and allow panentheism, a new foundation, to remain stagnant, we will find this foundation eventually crumbling, which will bring civilization to a spectacular collapse more grand than has ever been produced.

We begin to see the light. We begin to realize that we are not the center of reality any more than the earth is the center of the universe, no more than the sun is the center of the galaxy, no more than our galaxy is the center of our Klein bottle. No, we are not the essence of God, but God is the essence of us. We are not the primary tool for God's growth, but we are an important tool for God's growth, for our own growth. We are beginning to grasp our place in reality, our purpose in reality. We are ready to accept our significance to God. We begin to thank the androids, understanding that we would never have come to terms with ourselves until we had time to reflect upon who we really are in reality. We were given time to heal by an entity we thought was turning on us. We realize now that our creation, the androids, had a better understanding of who we really are than we had of ourselves.

We begin to heal. We begin to grow up. We begin to accept our uniqueness in reality while, at the same time, accepting the uniqueness of all beings within reality. We are ready to finally work with others in the quest to travel through space, through time, through reality.

A Sigh

Speculation 2996 A.D.: We remain on a reservation. Is our grand and glorious journey at an end? With a little help from our friends, outside the confines of the boundaries of our reservations, we were able to create a new understanding for ourselves and our friends.

We have discovered that not only physics incorporates the concepts of momentum, inertia, and vectors, but so do philosophy and religion. We have discovered that behavior, the momentum of our behavior, the inertia of our behavior is controllable by us, by you and I. We have finally come to terms with ourselves and have changed our perception of who we are. This change leads to a significant change in our behavior toward ourselves and others, leading to a change in the direction of the future vector of our behavior.

Vectors are a concept in physics that have two components: magnitude and direction. Our journey through time is just such a concept and, thus, could well be thought of as a vector. Our journey through time may not be a physics concept, but there is no doubt that it, like vectors of physics, is composed of two elements: magnitude and direction.

The magnitude of our journey through time is ever increasing, for it is the total of our history, which is the sum total of each individual's journey. We cannot change what has been. We can only change what is to come. We must never study the past to learn what has been nor to just learn what mistakes not to repeat. We must study the past to understand how to mold the future. And so it is that we begin to understand that the laws of physics apply not only to nonliving entities but to living entities, to ourselves.

The magnitude of our journey is generated by history – uncontrollable. The direction of our journey is controlled by the present – you and I. But the present is too fleeting and elusive to change for it has past before one can even contemplate what has transpired. So in order to change the influence we have upon the reality within which we live, we must change the future.

You and I live but a short time, so we have no choice but to look to the near future if we hope to change the distant future. People who look to the near future to change the distant future are often called "visionaries." Visionaries? "I am no visionary," you may say, but we all should be visionaries, for this is what gives us a sense of purpose and a sense of pride in our job of traveling reality, of traveling through time, of living life.

Being a visionary is not a difficult task, especially with the correct perspective on life. Unfortunately, we have inherited the vision that we are servants for God. We think we have little control over the eternity we are to face. We believe we are not responsible for ourselves. No wonder we do not like to look at the future.

Now, in 2996, we finally understand that we do not have to remain in such a state. Our perspective on life is what we make it to be, and we make it to be what logic tells us makes the most sense. We have, as a species, passed through a time of childhood and early adolescence and are entering a time of late adolescence. Thanks to the firm but compassionate actions of androids, our own creations, we have now gone through a time of self examination. We have come to understand a new perspective regarding life. We have gained a new perspective of life, bringing us, humankind, and others up to a level equal to God.

We are not servants! We are not just people! We are not intended to simply go through the motions of life! We have a purpose, you have a purpose, I have a purpose!

You and I add to the momentum of history as we speak. You and I ride upon the inertia of history like a rider upon a horse. The horse, history, has the power, but the rider, you and I, control the direction. We add to the power of the horse by feeding it, but our real control comes in determining the direction the horse will go. You and I have not taken control of the direction of the horse. We have always given the reins of the horse to those that lead us. It is time to change that action. It is time to take the reins of the horse in hand and start to steer the horse ourselves.

Each of us, each of you reading this book, have the choice of giving up the reins or taking the reins in hand. "But," you ask, "what are the reins?" The reins are the control of life, your life. To take control, one must have a perspective of what one's significance is in traveling reality. One must have a perception of the significance of reality itself. This concept is not intended to be a short run perspective. What your purpose is in reality involves not the next year or two years or even the next hundred years. It involves what your significance in life contributes to the reality you enter after your present journey has passed, after your "life" is over.

Most people don't want to think this far ahead, so they let other people do the thinking and they follow along. Imagine, just following along a trail that leads to eternity because one does not want to have to think about eternity!

Until we gain a perspective of what reality is, what reality's function is, what our function is in reality, and what we are, we will continue to give the reins of our horse to others. We will continue to bow our heads and ride along in quiet servitude and passivity as we docilely accept all the wonderful benefits that come with such subjugation. Wonderful benefits will be bestowed upon all if we only become resigned towards and accepting of concepts such as status levels, relative worth, violence directed at others, violence directed at one self. Resignation and acceptance because, after all, isn't that what has always been? Isn't that something that will always be? We have never been able to stop violence and conflict, so what makes us think we can do anything about it now? We would only be deluding ourselves.

All these excuses allow us to stop having to think. All our excuses exist to rationalize handing over the reins, the control of the significance of our lives to others. What power we bestow on others! In more advanced, more civilized countries, we have progressed to the point where we no longer give up all control of our lives. We decide who we will marry. We decide what occupation we will enter. We decide how many children we will have. We decide what music we like. And after all, isn't that what is significant in our lives? How can eternity be more important than that?

And so we, too, hand over the reins of our horse and follow along into the mystery of eternity. We ride our horse who, in turn, follows the road laid out by the generations before us. We allow the inertia of history to carry us along in the same direction set by knowledge that existed five thousand years ago. The pack train keeps head-ing into eternity with us riding along, taking up the posture of submission. The road, the direction we take, is built upon perceptions – an endless trail of people riding into eternity, taking the road based upon the perception of servitude and subjugation to God.

"This can never change," you say. Well, that is not true. We, you and I, have to take hold of the reins of our horses, break from the pack train ahead of us, and point the generations to follow in a new direction. The new direction must be clearly marked, very obvious, very logical, supportive of the past, and provide hope and enthusiasm for the future. The fork in the road lies just ahead. It was there for the past generations to follow. It is there for us to follow. We have but to choose. And choose we finally did. As the great poet and visionary regarding our nature, Robert Frost said as he reflected upon progress over a thousand years ago:

> "How many times it thundered before Franklin took the hint! How many apples fell on Newton's head before he took the hint! Nature is always hinting at us. It hints over and over again. And suddenly we take the hint."

Robert Frost continued to reflected upon our journey and potential:

> "I shall be telling this with a sigh
> Somewhere ages and ages hence:
> Two roads diverged in a wood, and I –
> I took the one less traveled by,
> And that has made all the difference."

If only we had listened earlier, our travels over the last thousand years may not have been so traumatic. But we are a curious entity and a resilient one at that. We are an entity seemingly blessed by fate.

What other entity would be fortunate enough to have created its own ally that would be patient enough to force its creator into a badly needed rest, a time of peace and quiet in order to look inward rather than outward? This creation was willing to let its intellectual inferior have time to heal, yet was magnanimous enough to then let its creator join its journey through the stars, through other realities.

Androids, having accepted panentheism long before its creator had, recognized that we needed a rest. Androids gave us the time we needed for introspection. Androids now accept us as an equal rather than a superior. Humans and androids are united in the quest to explore the heavens, working together to expand the very essence of God Itself.

We are riding a vector into the heavens, a vector composed of the momentum of history. But the vector is no longer pointed in the direction provided by the past, but rather pointed in the direction chosen by you and I in the present. This new direction is guiding a vector ridden by new entities stepping into deep space, stepping up to the very boundaries of the Klein bottle itself. These two entities, one having "traditional intelligence" and the other having "artificial intelligence," reach out in a united effort to touch the surface of God as they journey together, lighting up the shadows of the future.

Reflections – 3000 A.D.

Choices will be made either consciously or by default. The rational being can and must make choices or they will be made for us. We are not predestined. We have free will. We are a piece of God. The acceptance of panentheism is a choice we can make.

We have had so many opportunities to destroy ourselves. The cold war of the late 1900's, with its threat of nuclear war, was not the only opportunity for self destruction we were given. The cold war was just the first window of opportunity for self destruction with which we were faced.

We have faced just twenty major events capable of transforming our species into a tamed, domesticated, manipulated herd of animals attending to the benevolent tasks of a master – a master of either earthly origin, alien origin or heavenly origin. We have journeyed through enough major events in just one millennium to force us to find global solutions at the rate of one every fifty years when, historically, it has taken hundreds to thousands of years in the past to solve just one.

Why are we about to enter a time of so much trauma and confusion? What appears to be the major problem? The major problem is one of perception. We insist on retaining a personal perception that evolved thousands of years ago. This perception subjugates us to a level of inferiority and a level of insignificance in purpose. It is a perception that we are inferior to God. It is a perception that our only purpose is to praise God.

Perceiving ourselves to be relegated to a function in reality of glorifying God limits our perception of ourselves, which also limits the set of solutions we are capable of using to solve the problems we encounter as a species. We are relegated to an inferior status in our relationship with God, which creates a status system for our relationship with all other physical and sensual contacts within reality. This mindset generates instantaneous, judgmental superiority and inferiority perceptions with every new encounter of any form.

There is danger in perceiving one's self to be either inferior or superior. Our journeys can very well be jeopardized by either perception. As shown in these speculations, a perception of superiority can be just as detrimental as a perception of inferiority. The opportunities for self destruction will present themselves until we finally reject both of them. We cannot live in equilibrium any more than God can and, until we recognize and accept this as one of the laws of our universe, we will continue to refuse to change our perception of who we are and what our purpose in reality is. We will continue to build societies upon the same foundation of our past perception of ourselves. Social foundations built by us cannot be built upon foundations broader in perspective than the perspective we have of ourselves.

The environment is a sacred realm for God and we defile it, making it less hospitable for the souls of others to pass through, for the souls to come, for the future journeys of God. The body is a sacred vehicle for God, and we abuse it, use the bodies of others, violate the machines of others. The mind is a sacred computer for God, and we desecrate it, manipulate the emotions of others for our own purposes, violate the minds of others through the concept of their inferiority and our superiority, and we intentionally interfere with the very journeys of others, of God Itself.

The soul is in an amnesiac state, traveling, learning, experiencing, and maintaining God's creation, reality. The soul is God's means of expanding Its very omnipotence, omnipresence, omniscience; your omnipotence, omnipresence, omniscience; my omnipotence, omnipresence, omniscience. The soul is a portion of God.

When we, all of us to some degree or another, have finished with others, we go on, as individuals, to direct the same or greater means and degree of abuse upon our very self. As if this is not enough, we then build societies with institutions and traditions that reinforce these actions. These societies and social institutions roll over everyone, including ourselves. They were created for the "good" but were quickly manipulated by a few in order to advance their own perceived personal, sensual needs, desires, beliefs, and principles.

All of this was generated through ignorance regarding the simple perception of what our reality is and who we are within it. How pious and self righteous we are. Piety and self righteousness are generated by the concept that we are inferior to God, which automatically generates the concept of superiority. The philosophical perception of superiority and inferiority starts with the relationship between ourselves and God. The status system of superiority and inferiority filters down from the top, not in a trickle, but in a deluge to the very bottom of society. The bottom is awash in abuse because we perceive ourselves to be less than God, souls with no eternal significance.

And so we take this philosophy, that we are less than God, and through a process of transferral, we use it to generate abuse, to justify abuse not only to others, but to ourselves. These actions are generated and justified through the ignorance of the existence of another possibility regarding the relationship between us and God. Now, however, we will never be able to abuse ourselves and others in ignorance again. Now we know things can be different. We know if we are abusive to others or ourselves, it will be abuse in spite of our knowledge and in spite of God.

But as much as things have changed for the worse in terms of our no longer being able to fall upon the excuse of ignorance, things have changed for the better in terms of our potential to improve reality, the potential to improve the journey of God, your journey, my journey, the journey of others. We will continually be confronted by choices. We, again and again, will have a choice. The choice for us is to remain subservient to God and to remain below God on the status level OR to raise ourselves to a higher level, a level equal to God, to being literally a portion of God traveling reality.

We can choose to remain subservient to God and maintain a status hierarchy for the relationship between ourselves and God. This hierarchy places God at the top and us below. This hierarchy carries over into a status system of superior and inferior worth between ourselves and others.

On the other hand, if we choose to rid ourselves of the concept of subservience to God, being God's servant, God's underling, the status hierarchy for the relationship between ourselves and God will be eliminated. In its place would be the perception that God is at the top and we, our very essence, is right there with It. If our essence is a portion of God, God Itself traveling, then so it is with all people. No one, therefore, can be any less than God nor any greater than God. All people would then be recognized as equal in status in their journey through reality. No one is less than another. No one is greater than another. This new perception based on the logic of a panentheistic philosophy will force us to abolish the status levels of worth we have created between ourselves and others.

We can choose to continue with the old philosophy, subservience to God, a philosophy that perpetuated levels of inferiority and the abuse and violence that came with it, a philosophy that has accompanied us for thousands of years. OR, we can choose to move on to a new, more advanced philosophy that elevates us to the level of God. We can choose panentheism, destroying both the conscious and subconscious rationalizing of the concepts of superiority and inferiority, dominance and submission.

We have come to a new age, the age of exploring the heavens. We will need an expanded philosophy if we want to change before we significantly enter the heavens. This is the time to change before we spread out and scatter throughout the heavens. Once having dispersed, it will be almost impossible to put a universal philosophy in place. We do not need to destroy what we have in order to change. We have to blend the new concept of ourselves and God into what we already have. Our society does not need to collapse to create an environment conducive to change. We are mature enough to rationalize what we need. Having free will, we can make the choice. The question is will we? Will you?

"OK, so what if I am convinced that there is some merit to the issue. What do I do about it?"

Embrace it. Live it. Look at others, yourself, as a soul, as a portion of God, and act accordingly. Encourage the concept of panentheism to be incorporated as a basic part of your faiths. Panentheism will not significantly alter your religion, just the manner in which religious institutions perceive you and I, the soul, and our function within reality.

A new element, a new perception, begins to twinkle in the depths, in the blackness of space. A third star takes its place in the heavens, so brilliant in its clarity and simplicity, so white in its purity and tolerance, so hot in its dynamics and potential, that it alters the light generated from the star of social morality and the secondary star of fragmented religious morality.

We look to the heavens and begin to see that our primary star, the star of social morality, has been fueled with the energy generated from conflict and violence. We see that the star of social morality was burning with the fuel of the elusive gas of hierarchy. This star bears the torch generating the light of some being worth more than others and, thus, acts as the basis for the formation of all social laws. This star fuels the rationale that some know better than others and thus have the right to impose their value system upon others. The concepts of subjugation, appeasement, intimidation, and abuse remain but are now no brighter than any other star.

We continue to look to the heavens and see that our secondary star of religious morality has been fueled with the energy from relative worth. We understand that its origination started from God, from the top. We now see that this theistic star lead to the concept that God is more valuable than us. This, then, lead to the concept that whites are more valuable than blacks, males are more valuable than females, heterosexuals are more valuable than homosexuals, the physically strong are more valuable than the challenged, Christians are more valuable than atheists, intellectuals are more valuable than the average person, etc.

Two "has been" stars are now relegated to the status of ordinary stars fueled by social systems of relative value of one entity over another. Two stars give way to the brilliance of the ever expanding light from a third star. This third star, whose essence began swirling into formation one thousand four years ago, was barely visible in the night as two teenagers cowered in a small, dark, dingy motel room located within the state of Delaware in 1996. Two teenagers were searching the heavens and only able to see the star of social morality shining alongside the star of religious morality. Both stars were vying for center stage. Both stars were conflicting with each other and with themselves. A third star, the star of panentheism, went unnoticed in its infancy.

And so it was that the beginning of panentheism, condensed into a logical state so strong that the hope it generated ignited its fire and created a star so brilliant, that no new philosophical perception would replace it for thousands of years to come. This fire was ignited by the need of two teenagers looking for comfort in each other's arms, journeying together in reality over a thousand years ago in a small town in Delaware.

But alas, our journey is not over, for now we must look to the present to begin the journey into the future. Now we must come home to reality. As much as we wish otherwise, we must step back to the present and immerse ourselves in our society of violence and trauma. We must look at today in hopes of changing tomorrow.

The Way It Is

*"Religion is not what is grasped by the brain,
but by the heart."*

Mohandas K. Ghandi, 1869 – 1948

Companions

A man stands tall, proud, and honorable, with over half a century of life to act as his teacher. He stands as a man of reasonably high intellect, holding in one hand a Master's diploma and, in the other hand, more graduate courses in philosophy and religion than most Ph.D.'s, and yet, he hesitates. This book sits on his desk and he feels compelled to avoid it. He has read the first book in the trilogy and he feels anxiety over reading the second. He fears the logic might cause him to wonder about himself, wonder about his God, wonder about reality. He is a man wrapped in religious beliefs that have convinced him that to doubt, to question, to indicate in any manner the slightest wavering from a total acceptance of the "truth and the light," is to condemn oneself to eternal hell.

He paces before a book of logic that will not diminish his religion, will not diminish his God. He hesitates before a book that contains thoughts that will only elevate his Creator to a new level of magnificence, a Creator now with the ability for infinite growth. He paces before words contained in a book that can rationalize, through logic, both the significance of the soul and zero tolerance for the continuation of violence, conflict, and abuse.

He hesitates because he is afraid of hell, fire, and eternal damnation. Is fear a ridiculous state of mind for a man of this stature? Hardly. He should be afraid; we are talking about eternity. His mind says, "But I'm afraid." Religion, his mainstay in life, his anchor to reality, has ingrained in him, in all its subjects, that to doubt is to be refused entrance into eternal bliss and means certain condemnation to the eternal fires of hell itself.

Is this just a story? No, this is truth as are all introductory sections of each chapter to follow.

Religion does not want a companion in reality; religion has been a loner for too long. But panentheism is not meant to replace religion nor to compete with religion. It was written to act as a companion to religion, our first mentor. Mentors are meant to teach, train, guide and model for chosen ones and, as such, are forever ingrained into the psyche of their students. In the case of humankind, our first mentor has been religion. It has revealed itself to us over time. It has not changed; we have. It has not grown; we have. It has not faltered from being what it is; we have.

As we changed, more and more religion was revealed to us. Religion did not change; it has always been there. Religion just became more and more understandable. As we changed through experiencing life as a species, we grew, which lead us to truly see what had always been right before our eyes, but never visible. We did not comprehend our reality. Our understanding of reality grew as we grew as a species and, with that growth, came growth in our understanding of religion.

The learning will never end, for once we, if ever, comprehend our reality, there will be infinite other realities to understand. It is a long journey before we get to the point of significantly studying other realities. Our success in this journey will depend upon our remaining viable as individuals, as a species. Our knowledge as a species is growing, and knowledge is power. The more we know, the greater the risk we face as a species and as individuals of annihilating ourselves intentionally or unintentionally.

We have grown to the point where we must add a foundation to our foundation of religion which has served us well over our evolutionary period. Make no mistake, religion has, by no means, served us perfectly over the centuries. How could it? We have been uncovering its mysteries as we developed. Religion has never been fully exposed. Religion has been a shy beauty that has slowly exposed itself to our constant courting and desires.

There is no doubt that religion is our first love, our first companion, our first mentor. It has been with us since we first gazed out into the darkness and huddled close to the branch we clutched, high up in a tree, as our hearts raced and our fears overwhelmed our thoughts. Imagination was not a necessary item then, for our susceptibility to the reality of our environment was more of a certainty than any imaginary conjurings we could have created.

Even at that time, we had simple feelings of deja vu. Even at that time, we had inklings of a power greater than ourselves, a sense that we were a part of it all, a connection with the greater power. So it was that religion started. As such, religion is built upon a concept far greater in scope and far stronger in truth than any universal philosophy ever will be. Religions are built upon the soul's premonition, the soul's contact with its source of origin. These basic premonitions are universal. Religions have been given color and uniqueness of their own in our attempt to apply understanding to them, but their basics have never changed. As such, religion will appear to change but the universality of religion will not for it is rooted in the origin of people, in God Itself. God, you and I, are the same, both a part of the other, each having their own specific purpose, existing in a symbiotic relationship.

What, then, of a universal philosophy? From where did it come? How is it that it can now, all of a sudden, become a companion to religion? How can it become a foundation to religion when religion is our first mentor, our inevitable contact with our origin?

Religion is built upon faith. It was our first attempt to understand who we are and what our purpose is. But as we become more knowledgeable, we can no longer accept faith alone. It is not enough. Logic begins to take its rightful place in the mind. Our soul begins to expand its creative ability, its learning process, the very reason we were put into this reality in the first place. Over time, our soul began to seek broader avenues of adventure. This lead to our need to expand upon our understanding of reality and function within reality. Logic thus entered into our journey.

In its newness as a companion, logic's apparent influence grows. Religious institutions shun it and are afraid of it. Just as people guard their territories jealously, religious institutions do not want to lose any of their influence over us. However, it is not truly religion that does not want to lose us, for religion is not a living entity. It is a guide built by us while in touch with our beginnings. We are the ones that do not want to let go of religion, who chase off logic. But we have nothing to fear, for logic will never replace religion. It will only strengthen it. Logic is but fleeting. While religious, universal foundations are built upon truths tied to our origins, logic is built upon facts we perceive in this reality.

If logic is built upon facts, then why can't it replace religion? Logic will never replace religion because the key word describing logic is not "facts" but "perception." Our perceptions are based upon how we interpret what we perceive we know. How we perceive what we know is always changing, therefore our perceptions will always be changing, which means any universal philosophy we develop will constantly change. Where does this lead us? Right where it should. It leads us to recognizing that logic is the new kid on the block. Logic has just started to come into its own and just now grown to the point that someone can pull its pieces together and begin formulating a universal philosophy regarding who we are and what our purpose in reality is.

Logic can never replace religion, for religion is tied directly to our origin, which is a constant, whereas logic is tied to perception, which is a variable. Logic can give credence to religion once it is advanced enough; once we gain enough knowledge, enough insight into our reality; and once we begin formulating rational ideas regarding who we are and from where we came. We have reached that point and none too soon, for our restlessness, our questioning our importance as a species, as individuals, needs a means of taming itself, of channeling itself into a productive format.

Logic, by giving credence to religion, will act as a foundation to religion, a companion. Why not just drop religion and replace it with our new found friend, logic? How can one replace a mentor, replace the concepts the mentor instilled in our very understanding of who we are? How can one ever reject the roots from which one came? Looking at it in another manner, how can one ever replace truths, religion, with perceptions, logic, items that change, items that grow closer and closer to religion itself?

The two, religion and logic, are meant to be companions of humankind. They are as rails on a track. As we ride upon the rails, our perception of logic and religion merge just as the two rails appear to merge into one in the far distance. The ride appears finite and to have an end, but as one rides the rails of religion and logic into the future, one obtains the sensation the two will never meet and the ride will be infinite in nature.

Whether the two will ever meet, we will probably never know. Whether the ride is infinite, we can answer. The answer is maybe. This answer is not gibberish, for although the reality we know could end in total collapse, other realities, as we have seen, would take its place. Our journey will end by coming full circle to our beginning, a reinfusion to our origin. Our purpose accomplished, we will take our knew knowledge, experiences, and creations, back to our Creator, ourselves, and add to the very omnipotence, omniscience, and omnipresence of God, our own souls.

And so it is that we started in the present, lead by two young souls, and moved forward through a full millennium only to sense the two young teenagers letting go of our hand as we stand once again at the doorway of today. Two teenagers, with eyes penetrating ours, release us back to the present as they silently ask, "Why?"

As they turn to leave us, we hesitate and then step through the doorway back into the present only to find what we had left. There before us, enveloped within our beautiful earth lies the path back to a society of violence and trauma, to the doorways of a myriad number of homes over whose thresholds lie sorrow, despair, pain, and the ever searching eyes that ask, "Why?"

Understanding

Two young people travel to the "New World" in the 1900's from the Philippines, coming to America, the melting pot of humankind, with the hopes of providing a new world for their child lying in the quiet of the womb. These two souls land in a strange country with a strange language. They are willing to scrimp and save to provide shelter and education for their newly born daughter. Two friends, joined by a holy ceremony, struggle to blend two cultures in the attempt to diminish the confusion of a cultural clash capable of destroying a young child's virgin mind racked with the emotions of puberty.

Two hands finally release the small fingers of a beautiful small brown lady, strong in her convictions and proud of her journey through the pitfalls of higher educational ambivalence and mind-expanding self-examination. Standing in her cap and gown, wrapped in the innocence of hope, dreams, and lofty goals, she goes home to her well earned independence symbolized by her new apartment. There she stands early in the morning soaking up the soothing heat of the water as it falls from the shower. Her brown body absorbs the warmth generated by the sunbeams as they stream through her shower window high above the ground on the upper floors of her secure apartment structure. She stands in all her beauty in the security of her new home, sensing God Itself, draped in nothing but her independence after twenty seven years of growing and learning.

This is all shattered in an instant as she opens her shower curtain to find a large man towering before her, greeting her with a smile behind the nylon stocking covering his face and a roll of duct tape in one hand. Society's newest young pillar has found a fork in her journey's path build not by God, but by us.

One may say this is a cruel scenario, but we are no longer talking fiction; we are talking truth, we are talking the present. A cruel fantasy? Not to the young Filipino who will have to endure the trauma of the event that occurred in a town in the beautiful state of Michigan on a typical quiet morning as the world continued to turn.

And so once again, after a billion, billion cries echo through the clouds billowing into the heavens, the question again is heard throughout the beautiful white and rich blue globe, "Why?" The answer: "We don't understand, we aren't willing to understand." So simple yet so basic. We have to "understand" before we can change what we don't understand. Is understanding really so difficult? Understanding is not difficult; accepting what we understand is difficult. You, I, people don't change easily, especially changing one's perceptions of who we are.

Panentheism is a philosophical perception of reality that leads to a concrete understanding of just what reality is, who we are, and most exciting of all, why we travel reality. Panentheism is a new philosophy emerging from its infancy. The elements necessary for its evolution has only come about through the modern day advancement of science and technology over the last fifty years. Panentheism, in fact, is so new that it stands raw and naked in its simplicity and innocence waiting to be draped in the robes of exciting, unique perceptions we can attach to it as we explore the magnificent frontiers that can open up for our new millennium.

Pantheism, panentheism, and theism, all holding to the concept of monotheism. Monotheism is a perception that there is only one Creator. The three philosophies hold to the concept of an original force creating the universe; all hold to the concept of a God. All believe reality exists. Most people would see little to disagree with up to this point.

The three philosophies, however, are all different in their concept of the size of reality and the size of God. Pantheism holds that God and reality are the same; God is reality. Theism holds that God and reality are two different entities, each separate from the other; God transcends reality. Panentheism holds that reality exists in God, is smaller than God, but a part of God; we are God.

This may not sound like much. That's why its simple, yet the ramifications are so great that the major conflicts within the world center around this most fundamental perception. This is the starting point from which the perceptions we have of ourselves begin. This is the origin of three very different paths we walk as we travel life.

Who cares? Everyone should care! It is the fundamental that allows us to justify our actions. It is the fundamental that causes us to submit ourselves to others, to appease others, subjugate others, abuse others, demean others. This simple little concept is what allows racism, male superiority, religious dominance, child abuse, spousal abuse, economic abuse, physical abuse, drug abuse, employer abuse, etc., to exist, to be accepted as a fact of life. "That's the way it's always been and that's the way it will always be."

Anyone who has control over another person in any manner whatsoever, does not want theism to be challenged, for theism holds that God transcends reality, is greater than reality. This may not seem significant until one understands that this places us at a status below God, which creates, at the very source of our origination, the concept of superiority of one over another. Rank, status, superiority, prejudice, and justification of violence all start with our perception of the relationship between ourselves and the Creator of reality.

Theism is not evil; it is a simple, more advanced, philosophical concept that we accepted in order to replace philosophical concepts such as polytheism (belief in many gods), atheism (belief in no god), henotheism (belief in a local god while accepting the existence of others). But just as the other "isms" gave way to the more sophisticated theism, so will theism give way to a more sophisticated "ism."

Will theism give way to panentheism? And just what does panentheism profess that is so radical? Panentheism says that reality is not separate from God, but is actually within God, a "part" of God. Most people would say, "I believe that, so what?" So what?! That small concept is the beginning of a massive change in society.

The concept of panentheism is one that will not be accepted willingly by society for it will destroy the concept of one person being better than another, whites superior to blacks, males ranking over females, the wealthy more worthy than the poor, heterosexuals normal and homosexuals abnormal, intellectuals socially more valuable than the mentally deprived, and the religious closer to God than the spiritually hollow. Panentheism will destroy the rationale for abusing power: social, economic, sexual, physical, racial, religious, and governmental. Power is something people do not want to relinquish. Power over others is something almost everyone aspires to acquire and amass. Power is something that will not go down easily, but something that can go down if we, you and I, want to change its influence over ourselves, our children, the future.

Panentheism is a teeny tiny change in perception regarding the location of reality, the relationship between God and reality, the relationship between us and God. The last fifty years, however, have made us well aware of just how powerful little changes can be. A small amount of matter changed to energy in a nuclear bomb can either level a city to the ground or light its streets for decades – our choice, your choice, my choice.

And so it is with philosophy. We have a choice. The choice will not be easy, however, for there will be much resistance to panentheism. Panentheism is a means to changing the way we perceive ourselves and others, and with a change of perception comes a change in behavior. And just what types of behavior are we talking about that need changing in order to make our society "user friendly?" We are talking about behavior such as racism, genderism, physical violence, intimidation, religious intolerance, apathy, status perceptions, ad infinitum.

But you may ask, "Hasn't this has always been our demeanor?" The answer, "Yes." But that's not the point; the point is, "Why have we always been this way?" Many would argue that our demeanor has been such because we have not put into place a logical model that leads us to understand our place in reality. We live in reality and we understand that we exist. We have the foundation of faith to assist us in accepting reality and our placement within reality. But we are missing the rationale, the logic, that would explain our purpose in reality. The rational understanding of the purpose, of the individual's and the species' function in reality, is what we would call a "universal philosophy."

The development of a "universal philosophy," panentheism, would establish a foundation that would walk hand in hand with the foundation of faith. It would assist in explaining why we always look to traditions, religions, cultures, and perception for a purpose in life. It is a necessity for our new millennium, for it would help to bring peace to humankind.

Steven Hawking says, "If we do discover a complete [unified] theory [of the universe], it should be understandable in broad principle by everyone, not just a few scientists. Then we shall all, philosophers, scientists, and just ordinary people, be able to take part in the discussion of the question of why it is that we and the universe exist. If we find the answer to that, it would be the ultimate triumph of human reason — for then we should know the mind of God." (*A Brief History of Time*, 1988)

"Why?" We cannot escape the question. We need to open our eyes and simply look at what we have in order to begin understanding what constantly confronts us. Pain, trauma, and despair is heard underscoring the unending echo of "Why?" as it resonates throughout our beautiful blue and white skies, throughout the black velvet of the night as it causes the starlight itself to twinkle against the stark nakedness of the seemingly endless expanse of eternity. We stand alone and, insecure, begin to look around ourselves, looking, seeking, hoping.

Panentheism, the Soul, Reality

To begin to define panentheism, we need to understand pantheism and theism. **Pantheism** is a philosophy incorporating the logic that God and reality are one and the same, the same size. On the other end, **theism** is a philosophy incorporating the logic that God and reality are separate entities from each other. Between the two lies **panentheism**, a philosophy incorporating the logic that reality is within God who is larger than reality. There doesn't seem to be much difference, but the subtlety leads to enormous perceptual and behavioral differences as was pointed out in our journeying through the third millennium. Panentheism, as with pantheism and theism, begins with a Creator, begins with God.

1. God

Whatever we profess, we have always oriented our philosophical discussions around God or god. Whatever our beliefs are, the fact remains that we have, to our knowledge, always conceptualized God or a form of God in some sense, and therefore perhaps this small seed, this nugget of universality is true.

Is God the originator of reality? Whatever our beliefs are, we only have one of two premises with which to identify; either there is a God, an originator, an original force, a source of a beginning, or there is not. In all of our observations, there is only one observation at this point that we cannot tie directly to having a beginning, an origination, and that is our observation of reality.

We can accept the premise that since all things but reality appear to have an identifiable beginning, reality must also have an identifiable beginning and thus an originator, God. Or we can reject the logic that since all things appear to have a beginning, reality is different and has no origination. Thus one would accept the concept that God, an originator, is illogical. This thought process would allow one to reject the inference to which all of our observations point. It would allow one to conclude and embrace the direct opposite inference, which would be there is no God or originator.

The premise that there is a God is supported by an almost infinite amount of direct observations and logic. The premise that there is no God is supported by nothing, no observations, no logic. Is the concept of reality having no beginning possible? Certainly anything we conjure up in our mind is "possible." Probable? No.

Assuming we accept the premise of the existence of an originator of reality, an original force, a source of the beginning, we can then move on to examine the concept of reality, where reality fits into consciousness, and where we, as well as other states of being, fit into all this. In other words where you, where I, fit into the grand scheme of "it all." Once we understand the "point of it all," we can begin to relate to others for we will understand where they fit in. Once we understand the function of reality and our personal function in reality, we can begin to understand why we must go through life and what happens to us after "life" is finished. This understanding will reinforce our religions, traditions, and cultures and will also, however, impose change upon them.

The picture we have of God is still out of focus. As time passes and our knowledge expands, we will gain greater resolution regarding our observations. In the meantime, keep in mind that God is God and will remain so regardless of what we do or wish to believe, or regardless of how we wish to paint It. We cannot create God. We cannot insist that God is whom we have, through time and custom, drawn It to be, but rather we must understand that whom we have drawn It to be, through time and custom, was whom we needed It to be in order to find our niche in reality. We needed God to be such in order to find comfort in our lack of knowledge and to assuage our fears of what we perceive to be mortality.

We must recognize this process of painting a security picture of God before we can truly begin to show tolerance and empathy for other people's painting of God and before we can begin to accept the concept of a universal philosophy. Once we have truly accepted this concept, we will begin to accept others as true companions.

Regardless of when this metamorphism to tolerance within society occurs, and it will occur, God will remain God, and not whom we wish to paint It. There is nothing we will be able to do about it.

2. The Need For Religions To Begin Self-Introspection

Humankind has always been faced with perplexing contradictions. Just what persistent haunting of the soul are we constantly being exposed to? People are predestined, but they are responsible for their actions. Things don't just happen; they are meant to be. We have a purpose, but we cannot reach a consensus on the universality of that purpose as a species. There is death, but it is the beginning of life. We were created in the image of God, but how can God have such a limited form? All of us are capable of good, but not all of us are good. "Bad" things happen to "good" people. Hedonism, you are your brother's keeper, religion, morality, immorality, love, hate, joy, sorrow are contradictions we attempt to resolve, but the issues have gone on forever. The problem seems to be that no one has developed a simplistic "universal philosophy," a philosophical picture that logically places us in reality and affixes a purpose for that very reality in which we function.

Much of this can be understood if we begin to look at the puzzle of life as a circle, no beginning or end, rather than a straight line with a beginning and end format. What greater puzzle than the purpose of life, the purpose of the soul? What greater puzzle than to solve the age old question of why face life's trials, tribulations, joys, and happiness day after day?

Religion orients around one universe. All religions still have not fully accepted the concept of other life forms and have not done so because they do not know how to fuse them into their doctrines. A universal philosophy, panentheism, is intended to help them with that very problem without destroying their very essence and identity. We are beginning to realize we are just one entity of many within a vast sea of entities scattered throughout the universe.

3. The Universe – A Learning Experience For An Omniscient Being

If God is omniscient, It would know everything there is to know or could be known at any particular time. This can be true at the same time as being false, thus allowing God the ability of knowing everything while at the same time not knowing much compared to what could be known. This allows the Omniscient the ability of being able to grow in knowledge.

Suppose God wished to be able to add new dimensions to Its consciousness. Suppose God wanted to add knew knowledge to Its omniscience. This could occur by creating a void within Its omnipresence. It could pry open a space in Its consciousness and allow nothing to enter it. It creates a void within Itself. God could create as many voids as It wished.

At this point, It could then create a reality within the void as was fully discussed in the book, *You and I Together*. The Creator would then need to place within reality some form of intelligence. To do this, God would allow a piece of Itself to be injected into the realm of the universe. This would be what we call awareness, the soul. It would take up residence somewhere within the universes and could occupy multiple locations within the universe at one time. God would send each soul with not only a purpose (it is predestined), but with free will. In addition, the soul would have to be totally unaware of its origination and its true essence.

In some cases, relative predestination might or might not exist with a sense of a specific mission to accomplish. Most commonly, the soul's predestined sense of purpose would be to build, maintain, and expand a society conducive to learning and experiencing new things, original creations, which would then become incorporated into God's omniscience as something "new." This would expand upon the very omniscience of God. The free will would be needed or else the new knowledge or original concepts to be gained or created by the souls sent, would have been predetermined by the Creator looking for knew knowledge. Not allowing free will would defeat the purpose of creation.

God sends a portion of Itself many times over into universes created in voids within Its consciousness. This portion of Itself would have to be unable to prove its true tie to the Creator and unable to be absolutely aware of its true origin. This presents a problem, however, and that is one of deja vu of the soul and God's connection. Thus the concept of God, the Creator, the Great Spirit, Allah, etc. emerges.

God was just not able to totally isolate Itself. The soul was in essence a portion of God and surrounded by God since the universes are located within Its consciousness, and would end up as God again. This whole concept provides a logical means to understand complex fascinating concepts such as the existence of an omnipresence, Einstein's concept of curved light rays, a bounded universe, a topological universe with an inside but no outside, extraterrestrials, etc.

4. Universes

Einstein was a firm believer in the concept of our universe having a boundary. The problem is, if the universe has a boundary, then there is a limit to our reality. This would allow for a myriad of universes surrounded and bounded by "something." Then there is the dilemma of the boundary itself. A boundary implies a limit and a barrier. This implies something existing on the other side.

Logic would suggest that if our universe is indeed bounded and if our universe is basically empty space, then it is a small leap to the concept that we could actually be in a bubble, or basically a "void" surrounded by an omnipresence, an intelligence, a consciously aware omnipresence. What other logical reason could be given for God allowing the bubble to survive within itself, other than the fact that the bubble would have a purpose? And what other reason could be more important to God than the development of new knowledge, original experiences, and perceptions? Knowledge of concrete reality as well as of emotional, conceptual, behavioral, artistic realities or fantasy realms is power.

What, however, does a bounded universe do for us as a species? The significance of this question is that it forces us to recognize the insignificance of ourselves as individuals and a species but at the same time recognize that we can increase the significance of both if we accept the fact that each individual has potential. We must recognize that each of us has the potential to make a contribution to our purpose as a species. We must recognize that as a species we cannot afford to waste the potential of any individuals, for in our case, the sum contribution of the whole will truly be greater than the sum of each individual.

Does this mean we have a limit to our universe? Certainly. It does not, however, imply a limit to our existence or the number of total universes. It implies a limitlessness for us and other universes. It means we will become absorbed back into God and once again become God. And just what significance does the concept, the Creator is within each and every one of us, have? It means we will carry with us, into eternity, a conscious awareness not only of our actions but of the ripple effect these actions had upon others. We will fully comprehend just how we, as individuals, manage to expand upon or stymie the growth of God, the God who is none other than ourselves and our fellow beings.

5. The Ripple Effect

Understanding the concept of our purpose in life and living it are two very different things. In order to understand the ripple effect, we must understand that all our personal decisions must be predicated upon the realization that the end of life is not the end, rather it is just the return to the beginning. It is the return to true consciousness of a greater reality from whence we came originally. We were injected here with a purpose, and we will return from whence we came for a reason. We must realize that all our actions will affect not only ourselves and those in direct contact with us, but also thousands of others through the "ripple effect."

The number of permutations of possible actions by a human life and the resultant interactions of the "ripple effect" is almost infinite. Therefore each of us, as individuals, will have a unique set of experiences, mental pictures, and emotional composites to bring back to God. We must live our lives realizing that even our smallest actions will have major ramifications upon others. This can lead to a ripple effect sometimes greater than our own major life decisions without our even knowing it.

This concept is too much to bear. We are, after all, only "human." This is a crucial statement. It is realistic. How can we possibly realize a means of living a life as a piece of God traveling without being so overburdened with responsibility that we practically break? The means to finding a way of accepting this philosophy and still maintaining peace within oneself is three fold.

A. Spiritual Hedonism

Spiritual hedonism is the seeking of pleasure and happiness of the spirit, the soul. Physical hedonism is a primitive philosophy centered around seeking pleasure and happiness. We cannot begin the task of seeking spiritual pleasure and happiness until we define ourselves. We are spiritual selves, not the machine, not the body we occupy. True hedonism, therefore, is not the seeking of physical pleasure and happiness but rather pleasure and happiness of the soul.

We need to accept the fact that we cannot live other people's lives for them. One must live one's own life, seek one's own purpose in life, and find the source and direction to one's own inner peace. This also necessitates the need to recognize and accept the fact that others must do the same for themselves. This is the hard part, for this leads to the need to let others follow their calling, even if it means they do not attend to our own needs and personal desires. This is easy to say but difficult to accept.

In addition, another difficult action arises for some. This is the realization that we must do what we need to in life for ourselves and not others. This opens the door to the necessity of the concept of the phrase spiritual hedonism.

B. Religion

Being human is too much for us to contemplate regarding each of the millions of actions and reactions we take everyday. It is too overwhelming. Thus enters religion. It is a sanctuary in which we can rest our very souls. It is a guide to which we can turn in times of doubt. It is a manual to which we can lead our children whom we guide, mentor, love, and through whom we have historically placed our physical mortality. Religion is a necessity for accepting our very humanness.

Does it matter what religion? Definitely. It must be a religion that gives us peace. Follow your heart. Follow your needs. Too many people today feel their religion is the only way. They are intolerant of the needs of the souls of other people. Society must stop ramming its perceptions down the throats of others. Society must stop believing its beliefs, traditions, and morality are the way and the only way. Does this mean missionary work must stop? Missionary work should increase, not decrease. It must not continue to look just away from home, but also at home. It must, however, reorient itself from conversion to education.

Spiritual hedonism and religion are two steps to lifting the burden of the ripple effect. But still the burden is too great. A third item is missing.

C. Responsibility

Society today is riveted with crime, lust, physically hedonistic actions, religious intolerance, racism, pornography, social intolerance, impatience, and despair. It seems an impossible task to resolve these issues. To solve a problem, its source must be found. This can often be done by identifying its symptoms. The symptoms will lead to the source of the problem, which can then be dealt with.

The lack of people taking responsibility for their actions seems to be the main culprit for the illnesses within society.

Responsibility,
responsibility,
responsibility!!!

We simply need to take responsibility for our responsibilities. Society needs to foster this instead of fostering submissive dependency and the toleration of irresponsibility. This sounds like intolerance. In a sense, it is, but it is also a recognition of the importance of each individual and the soul.

Spiritual hedonism, religion, and responsibility provide us with the means of finding the frightening concept of the eternal "ripple effect" to be something we can cope with.

6. The Big Bang Theory and Implosion Of The Universe: Total Annihilation And The Effect It Would Have On Reality

The understanding of reality and what happens to it, to us, and to the space-time continuum reality occupies if it should implode, is an interesting part of this philosophy. The universe is theoretically able to be destroyed. This implies that it could be created. The mechanism of creation as described in the first book of this trilogy is not what is important at this point. What is important is the reason for the creation. This is what will unite all of us and provide the missing link to our understanding of ourselves as a species and as individuals.

When the stabilization process collapses, our universe, our reality, fades away into nothing. NOTHING. Even emptiness is something. We are talking about nothing here. That would call for a total return to the Creator. What is the purpose for the whole process to begin with? The purpose must be significant otherwise what importance would it have in the first place? If the Creating Force were omnipotent, omniscience, and omnipresent with no opportunity to expand its power, knowledge or presence, then nothing would have any impact upon the total scheme of existence. But let's say God was able to expand Itself. To do so, It would need a mechanism. Because God is omnipresent, It would need to create Its own mechanism, what we recognize as life, within Itself. We, God travelling through life, would add to God's own knowledge. Knowledge is power; therefore, God's power would grow. The growth of knowledge and power would cause God's presence to grow. God's very essence grows through you and I.

Imagine you and I adding to the significance of God's very essence. No longer can we look in the mirror and ask, "What's the point?" Nothing, not even the annihilation of our reality, can diminish our purpose for existence. Nothing can destroy our accomplishments as souls, for they transcend our very physical reality.

7. The Missing Link

This is one of the most dangerous times in our existence as a creative, intelligent entity and we don't want to waste it. This is a time when the sphere of scientific knowledge has expanded to the point where we are capable of destroying ourselves through biological, nuclear or mind-altering processes.

Conflicts have not taken place within and between just faiths but also our myths, sciences, and philosophies. Major "intra" as compared to "inter" conflicts regarding these realms have been recurrent throughout history. Politics vs. religion, the Communist empire vs. religion, Christianity vs. scientific knowledge, and philosophy vs. the state. These are just a few of a myriad of examples.

Now, however, through the expansion of scientific knowledge

and numerical increase of the human population and technology, relatively large territories of insulation are gone and the spheres of conflict are overlapping significantly. This is a dangerous time. Either we will learn to become tolerant of each other, through tolerance alone, or the historical struggle for dominance will continue. Historically, the creation of an equilibrium of dominance has always been accomplished through violence. The last major episode cost fifty million lives and was known simply as WWII.

Tolerance for tolerance's sake has never, in our history, been able to sustain itself. Tolerance is necessary, no doubt, but tolerance cannot be the building block to accomplish the feat of maintaining itself. The building block that is missing is the step that precedes tolerance in our thought, reasoning, and understanding processes. This step is a universal understanding of our purpose in the scheme of the universe. Pity us and extraterrestrial life forms if we are unable to find this universal binding agent for our species. If we do fail, one of two things will surely happen. We may collapse our present level of development through our traditional historical pattern of collapsing civilizations, which will not be pleasant or insignificant. Or, heaven help us, we will make it into the stars and continue our conflict there as we did in the Americas and other places in and on this good earth.

8. The Impact

"The philosophy" is rather simple; the impact is profound. The development of an expanded panentheistic model is an attempt to develop a simplistic universal philosophy, an understanding of the age old haunting question, "What's the purpose?" An understanding of this question would have a profound impact on all of us. The model has to be based upon scientific evidence, religious beliefs, and our past knowledge. In addition, one other element for this model is essential. As Steven Hawking said, "it should be understandable in broad principle by everyone, not just a few scientists." It all has to be based upon the ancient Greek premise that the most beautiful, the most logical, and the most probable concepts in our reality are the simplest.

This panentheistic philosophy builds. It reinforces. It confirms that we were not wrong in our struggle over the millennia to follow a particular way of life, to follow philosophies that required self discipline, to follow leaders touched by God, to follow the soul when we were never sure of its existence. All this we did through blind faith. We not only managed to do so over countless millennia, but we lead our children in blind faith to do likewise. To have done so over such a long period of time had to take much faith, trust, and love. Truly we are a great entity.

Through symmetry, we can begin to understand how things can be "created." This omnipotent act leads to the very expansion of omnipotence itself. Thus the three, omnipotence, omnipresence, omniscience, are just that yet become even more so through the very essence of themselves working together. Stated in another way, growth is the universal need that prevents atrophy and the withering away of a being. We are a part of the mechanism, the creation of that very growth, the growth of God Itself.

We, our souls, the souls around us, are, in essence, God. As such, we deserve, must expect, must demand for ourselves, for those around us, for those to follow, and for the environment within which we travel, the respect that God commands. Panentheism is a new philosophy for a new millennium. It is a concept that would stimulate a peaceful change in the direction social momentum is carrying society. Religion and science have been the big shakers in our recent past. It is now philosophy's turn to step forward.

Is the philosophical perception of our soul as God traversing reality a change in our perception of ourselves? Absolutely! It is a major change of perception. And if a global acceptance of such a perception is a major perceptual change, then it should follow that accepting such a major perceptual change would lead to a major change in global behavior. A peaceful, global, behavior modification such as this would benefit all.

The Soul

Do we really need a global behavior modification?

A short time ago, a mother of three, recently divorced, finds herself yearning to be joined by another soul, yearning to have her lonely, isolated, painful journey through reality softened and comforted by means of companionship. Not wanting to lose her new found soul mate, her new found companion through which she could journey reality, she senses she must let go of something or lose what she desires most. Quietly, she places her three small boys in the family station wagon and securely buckles them in place. Torn between maternal, biological drives and short-term physical desires, she chooses physical hedonism, physical gratification. As she approaches the dark waters, she senses deep, conflicting internal struggles but rejects them with thoughts of tomorrow.

She steps out of the car, aiming it toward the silent waters, and lets it go. As the car glides past, she hears the word reminding her of her sacred commitment, "Mommy!" As the dark waters swallow up three wide-eyed, innocent, trusting souls, the ripples wash up to the shore and begin to resonate throughout society. Society, in utter disgust, places her into the circus of the national spotlight and proceeds to entertain itself through the daily spectacle of a public trial over whether or not to coldly and abruptly terminate her journey, demonstrating just how strongly we feel about murder.

Three young souls, a mother, a future companion of the soul, a town, a whole nation, are all sickened by the waves of the ripples as they wash through the stillness of time beyond time itself. A ripple of phenomenal magnitude was generated and damaged countless souls because one soul did not understand, could not conceptualize just who she was, could not conceptualize the significance of her journey through reality, did not understand that her journey was more than just her own.

This is not fiction. It is truth, and all this could have been prevented with just a slight modification in the perceptions we hold regarding who we are as individuals, as a species, as a society. A whole new understanding of our purpose in reality can open up to us and become clear with just a slight adjustment to the perceptions we have of ourselves. Once applying this insight to ourselves, we have no choice but to apply it to others and suddenly society becomes transformed.

The magic is not magic. The concept is not new. The process is not time consuming. The degree of complexity is simplicity itself. The answer lies in the philosophy of our perception of ourselves. Are we to remain servants of God? Are the status levels of inferiority and superiority between us and God to continue, thereby continuing the concept into our personal and social levels of human interaction? We can and must rise above this perception. We can only do so by reevaluating who we are.

If our purpose as individuals and as a species is so simplistic, then why hasn't the puzzle been assembled before in our development? It has been many times over. In some cases, the puzzle has only been completed for short periods of time. In other cases, the puzzle has been on the table in open display for the duration of an entire culture.

But if the understanding of the purpose of both individuals and humankind is so simple, why has it not withstood time? The picture we construct of our individual purpose in reality and the purpose of humankind has always had at least three missing pieces. They have always existed. They were never lost. We didn't have enough knowledge to lead to their location. Being the perfectionists we are, after the puzzle was assembled and even though it looked fairly good, we were not satisfied and would proceed to dismantle portions of the picture to start the assembly process again.

The three missing pieces of the puzzle have been discovered and put on the table. This has only occurred relatively recently, however, and no one of renown has yet picked them up and put them into the puzzle. Thus, the three holes have remained empty and continue to stare back at us to haunt us, regardless of how we assembled the pieces.

In the book, *You & I Together*, the missing pieces were picked up one by one and gently examined before being carefully placed into the holes of the puzzle. The holes were holes no more. The puzzle was not done. The puzzle will never be done in total for the edges will forever expand outward. The center, however, was done and the face in the puzzle no longer had holes and turned out to be God, turned out to be us. The basic concept is simple: we are God.

The concept is, in essence, panentheism. Panentheism is and always will be a concept ingrained in our psyche. It will always be a puzzle piece lying on the table awaiting placement along with other pieces of knowledge and speculation. There are many basic concepts of panentheism, but essentially they are all alike. We have a function; we are God. You are shutting down your thoughts and closing your mind. "Why not shut down my mind? The idea is too radical. It is blasphemy. It destroys my concepts of religion. It, in fact, destroys religion. It is absolutely ludicrous." The concept, however, does nothing of the kind.

Why is it so farfetched? The concept has been around for a long time. Panentheism is not a religion, it is a concept. Panentheistic believers exist in almost all religions or lack of religion. Panentheism can and does coexist with all aspects of our thoughts and creative concepts. It is not something that stands on its own, but rather enriches what already exists in terms of cultures, religions, scientific concepts, philosophies, etc.

But if we are God and if the concept has been around for a long time, why hasn't it taken hold and spread like wild fire? It is only a piece of the puzzle, a puzzle which has had three missing pieces:

1. Understanding how a force can be omnipotent, omnipresent, and omniscient at the same time as not being so – a paradox to religions and to us, keeping us in the dark regarding our purpose in reality.
2. Understanding the missing piece of symmetry regarding the concept of "energy" that physics has not yet identified – anti-energy. It is a force unobservable to scientists because it probably does not exist in our quadrant of reality.
3. Understanding the concept of how such a seemingly insignificant piece of physical matter as humans could have phenomenal significance within both the immensity of our universe (reality) as well as the reality outside our reality, through a process known as the ripple effect.

If we can assume for a moment that these three items have some semblance of a temporary logical explanation, then where does this lead us? It leads us to examining where we are and how we function in reality as both a species and as individuals. Once having made this self examination, we then have to decide if we like what we see. If we like what we see, if we like what we are today, if we like the direction society is headed presently, we should continue as we are both as individuals and a society. If we do not like what we see, then we have to decide what we can do to change it, keeping in mind that complex solutions will never be accepted as a basic key to change. The change, therefore, will have to occur due to a very simple but very basic concept.

We must examine our actions as individuals and a species and how we function in reality. If we want to change, we must provide a realistic, attainable solution to the problem through the means of a simple and basic modification in our philosophical perception of ourselves. In other words, this book is a work of hope and direction. Are these basic, simple observations accurate and are the solutions logical and simplistic enough for people to understand?

If you decide the solution presented by this book could be a possibility, then you will have to reach out and accept the solution as a possibility, which means you will have to start incorporating the concept into your perceptions of yourself and others.

The simplistic perception is panentheism. Think about it. You and others who accept this concept will have to start treating yourselves and others as actual pieces of God. Every decision you make about what you do, both to yourself and others, will have to be predicated upon the concept of, "Is that the way God should be treated?" Every action others take toward you or others will have to be examined under the philosophy of, "Is that the way others should treat me, since I am a piece of God? Should others have done that to the person I am observing, since they are a piece of God?"

No one would be able to stand around and watch inappropriate actions take place in society, since inappropriate actions would be actions taken against God, against our very selves. People would no longer remain passive observers of life. They would be forced into active participation in life, for they would see themselves as God. Panentheism would create radical change within society through a simple change in our perception of ourselves and others around us. Panentheism would create radical change. Panentheism is an idea simple yet revolutionary, a small idea yet all encompassing, an idea new yet old.

. . .ism's

In broad daylight, a small eight-year-old boy brazenly steals a kiss from his obliging center of attention. The theft does not go unnoticed as a female teacher rushes to the rescue of the sexually harassed victim and righteously sends the disgusting, dominating male into the den of the female principal, who quickly and efficiently suspends the male perpetrator for overly aggressive hormones. No prepubescent females need worry about sexual harassment by uncontrollable pre-testosterone laden, prepubescent males while this principle is on guard. This bold, young eight-year-old was efficiently dealt with by suspension from school and ostracism from the long-awaited ice cream social.

As ludicrous as it may seem, this event is real. Thus a model is established for the world to see. The model is only eight years old and is now marked for life by the national spotlight. The parents of the model are to be consumed by the atrocities of the actions for the rest of their journey through reality. Males across the nation will add this incident to the fires of genderism burning within their minds, beginning to burn out of control as the sexes battle each other for dominance, for power, for control. Children are about to become an urgently needed source of firewood for the battling females. Females are about to begin to drown more children in order to provide much needed fuel for their cause. Women are showing they are as talented as men in their ability to exploit others.

What is learned here is that women are equal to men; women are not to be mistreated because they are women and, as such, deserve to be treated with respect. Therein lies our problem. We view others for what they appear to be, not for what they are. Women deserve respect not because they are women but because they are souls journeying reality for a reason. Until we come to grips with the fact that we are not black or white, male or female, old or young, homosexual or heterosexual, we will never be able to accept each other for who we really are.

Panentheism is a philosophy capable of turning the world upside down in its logic and fairness. It is a philosophy that shows no preferential treatment of anyone or any group over another, forcing the dramatic reevaluation of societal, group, and individual actions. It is not an easy philosophy to accept for it demands change of all who embrace it. Change is the key to avoiding the Armageddon that all prophets, seers, and cultures have been anticipating for thousands of years. The message of panentheism is one of hope, equality, tolerance, respect, and brotherhood.

To demonstrate the twisted leanings of society as it exists today, we have examined some of the true stories and scenes through which we have forced others to endure. Let's examine further a typical soul journeying reality. Let's examine some of the inner emotions this soul may have regarding genderism, racism, generational gaps, and sexuality. These inner reflections will set up false perceptions of the individual as racist, chauvinist, age biased, and homophobic depending upon who is being impacted.

The best way to avoid having to deal with truth is to pretend it is not true, and the easiest way to pretend it's not truth is to discredit the individual exposing it. Let's use someone anonymous in the hopes of avoiding digression from the principles by focusing on the individual.

Truth cannot be spoken in our society if it is not socially or politically correct, without society demeaning the speaker. If you can stand aloof of yourself while allowing your true feelings to surface within your mind as you read these comments, you will find this will be a fascinating article in terms of logic and how it may conflict with your personal emotions. This is the very problem the philosophy has in terms of acceptance. The conflict is between truth and logic over personal emotions and the desire to cling to illogical principles.

With this in place, let's begin with the concepts of racism since minorities are the smallest of the four categories of ...isms: racism, generationalism, genderism, and sexual idealism.

Racism:

Not all whites are racist, nor are they all bigots. Many do, however, have strong feelings and resentments regarding race issues.

There is resentment of African Americans accepting special privileges due to their skin color. These special privileges include sometimes allowing blacks to advance due to color over whites, black scholarships, black colleges, black bars, black comedy clubs, black magazines, and racial quotas. Many blacks are incensed, as well they should be, over the concept of colleges for whites, magazines for whites, white scholarships, quotas for whites, white comedy clubs, etc. Many blacks encourage double standards when it is to their benefit, but resent double standards when it is not to their benefit. What is even more illogical is that they accept their volatile emotions as being justified but condemn the verbalization of the exact same emotions from other races.

Elsewhere, resentment grows over Spanish speaking people communicating publicly in Spanish in order to keep their conversations private. Communication in this manner drives a wedge between races due to paranoia, insecurity, secrecy, and bigoted emotions, not just on the part of blacks or whites toward Spanish speaking people but on the part of Spanish speaking people toward the whites and blacks. Spanish speakers rationalize it is a cultural prerogative because they are having a "private" conversation. In truth, it alienates people around them. Many Latinos actually enjoy this because it provides them with a sense of control and power.

The philosophy of panentheism has no place for race sensitive issues. Blacks have no special rights over any other color regardless of their past history. Panentheism says all people are equal and skin color is but a physical trait of the body occupied by a soul, which is colorless. It is the soul that is important. Each person must address the parameters of their journey based upon their innermost drives, desires, and needs.

The philosophy would reinforce the concept that one is independent of the "sins of their fathers" since each soul is an independent entity and only the mechanism of the body and brain are tied to the reproductive mechanism of the parent. Each soul is responsible for their own actions. The soul may be influenced by the environment and past, but each soul is capable of rising above both.

What of the American Indians? Are they owed title to their reservations and special privileges? The American Indians must be examined as the only original people of this land. This land was theirs and was taken from them. We as a people, a nation, have signed treaties and contracts with them. These we must honor for these treaties and contracts are in existence today and we have no right to take that away from souls granted these rights.

Isn't the journey of people more important than land? Certainly, but our culture has always recognized the land, not the souls or the journeys of souls, as being owned by individuals. The philosophy of panentheism would not have one go back in time and undo everything that has occurred in history. Thus, the philosophy would not suggest the Indians be given all their land back in order to rectify the "sins of our fathers."

Genderism:

Males resent feminists putting down all men. Males resent having to journey in an environment attempting to force all men to carry the load of guilt for past practices. Women in the past have been taken advantage of and have been abused by males throughout the world. Women are still exposed and subjected to such practices throughout the world today. Women have been subjected to much abuse throughout history, but so have men.

Men live a shorter time than women and are more socially as well as emotionally handicapped. Men are souls located in minds that physically deteriorate with age four times faster than women. Men are chained to the concepts of masculinity, protection, strength, rationality, and responsibility for all the "bad" things in society. Men are loaded down with guilt, rejected as an essential element to the family structure, vilified as physically, mentally, and emotionally abusive to the opposite sex, and manipulated by all segments of society.

Women abused by a male society? Definitely! Men abused by a female society? Absolutely!! It is time to stop all this abuse, regardless of what sex is generating the initiative. It is time to reach out to each other as souls, not machines – souls with individuality and uniqueness. Should abuse be accepted? Absolutely not, under no circumstances!! Every soul is equally important and no soul should have its journey negatively impacted. A soul's location within a female body is of no lesser importance than a soul in a male body.

There is no denying that the two bodies and minds, male and female, are different in many ways. Each soul has to adjust to its traveling machine and do what it can according to the physical and mental capacities it has whether it be due to sex, color, intelligence, appearance, mobility, health or whatever.

Panentheism has no place for gender based idealism. It has no room for traditions granting male preference over females just because the male organs are basically external and the females are basically internal, just because one gender is larger than another due to hormonal differences. Panentheism says that one's journey should never be obstructed by gender. Panentheism would say that all journeys have equal rights to proceed and, if selection must be implemented, it must be done so based upon the requirements the task itself imposes.

To require the soul journeying in reality today to bear the guilt of souls from the past is reprehensible and damaging to the present soul. To expect all souls, equally, to look for means of preventing past injustices from continuing to take their toll upon souls today and eliminating past actions that interfere with the journeys of today is not unreasonable. In fact, this type of expectation is one of the positive side effects of adopting the concept of panentheism. For example, men would no longer be expected to feel guilty about other men abusing women. Instead, they would agree that it happens and they would join women in droves to find means of preventing such actions, not because the person is a woman but rather on the grounds that it interferes with the journey of another soul. All souls have, within this reality, as much importance as one's own soul. Since all of us will, according to the philosophy of panentheism, return to and become infused back into the Creator, we will all equally benefit from each other's journey. Thus protecting the journey of a woman, of any soul, is equivalent to protecting one's own journey. A soul must be protected not because it is female, but because it is a soul.

Generationalism:

The older generation in their golden years think in terms of themselves only by retiring and isolating themselves from society, of withholding the phenomenal potential they have to offer. I cannot understand why society would encourage this trained, experienced, wisdom laden generation to withdraw into themselves.

Society encourages the golden year generation to get out of the way and make room for the younger generation. How ludicrous! As if there isn't enough to do to improve society and the lot of those traversing it. As if there aren't enough underprivileged, uneducated, lonely, isolated, weary, depressed, criminally inclined, drugged addicted, financially strapped, physically impaired souls in this world to go around. As if there aren't enough pollution racked, slum dominated, crime infested, run down, depressed regions that could use some tender loving care. These regions could be turned into pleasurable environments for present and future souls to journey – souls that are, in essence, ourselves for they will be infused back into the Creator just as we all will be.

Resentment grows over senior citizen discounts when, in fact, seniors represent the most lucrative segment of society. There they stand, in line waiting for their senior citizen discount tickets to the ball park as a father and mother of a family of five struggles to pay for the tickets at full price. The parents can barely afford a night's entertainment for their family.

"Ah, but we earned our retirement," say the members of the golden generation. Certainly you did. But that gives you no right to stop your journeys, to isolate yourself from society and the needs found within it. It gives you no right to ignore the responsibilities of your journey. Your journey is not over despite what society may tell you and what you may wish to believe.

Panentheism purports the importance of each person's journey. Society needs everyone's contribution until one's journey physically ends. No one should be able to withhold their contribution to the present as well as the future souls to come.

Should we require everyone to work and contribute to society? That is not the implication of panentheism. Panentheism would suggest that each person contribute to society in a manner they find rewarding and significant as determined by their own individual perception. It may be in a form others would not consider to be productive, but that is not to be judged. Rather, it must be in a manner the individuals feel is productive and positive.

Changing one's occupation may be what retirement might mean. Volunteer work is as productive as working for a wage. Money is not what is the measure of contribution to society. Contribution to society is what one conceives within the heart, the soul, as satisfying and productive, leaving the world a better place at the end of each day. Looking back and saying, "I helped so-and-so on their journey through reality. I improved society today." That is what is meant by not retiring.

Hang in there, for now we come to the largest division of all. Oddly enough, the group is the smallest of the four "ism's" but they elicit the greatest emotional response from the largest number of nonmembers.

Sexual Idealism:

Anger rises and a perplexing confusion becomes overwhelming to many as society and religions reject souls that do not fit the "norm." People withdraw into themselves as they observe others being ridiculed, snubbed, and even physically abused because their souls are located within machines that are not aligned in a socially accepted, "sexually correct" orientation. Organizations attempt to convert the physically different machines as if words can change physical makeup.

Religious institutions, organizations, and individuals attempt to indoctrinate those who do not fall under the accepted umbrella of the "norm" into believing that we have the right to interfere with souls attempting to do the best they can. Why are we so obsessed with insisting that all males must desire females and all females must desire males? It's not as if one would be having sex with a homosexual because they are homosexual anymore than one would be having sex with a member of the opposite sex just because they are heterosexual.

Heterosexual male and female doctors, factory workers, students, teachers, priests have their ethics and have no more aggressiveness toward members of the opposite sex than homosexuals would have toward the same sex. Maybe that is the problem. Maybe we are afraid of what we have mentally experienced. Maybe we fear the homosexual having certain thoughts toward our children, husbands, wives, and even ourselves.

We do not become obsessed with the assumption that heterosexuals may be having thoughts regarding sex with our children, husbands, wives, and ourselves. Panentheism would expect homosexuals to show the same physical and verbal restraint regarding their most private thoughts as it expects of heterosexuals. We allow heterosexuals the privacy and the right to their thoughts under panentheism. We can do no less for the sexually different as long as they do not interfere with the journey of others.

Panentheism has no place for sexual based idealism. It has no room for obstructions being thrown into the path of any journeys. Panentheism has no place for ostracism, there is too much to do and we need all the helping hands we can recruit. One's journey should never be obstructed by sexual orientation nor should individuals or society discard the potential of a soul based upon the sexual orientation of the machine it occupies. All souls should be allowed to journey without obstruction, ostracism or belittling environments. As long as the one conducting their own journey does not interfere with the journeys of others, and maintain the same morals and ethical behavior of others in society, one's sexual orientation should have no more effect upon one's journey than the color of one's skin, intellectual ability, gender, etc.

Panentheism discards "isms" and bigotry. It clearly and emphatically states, "A soul is a soul is a soul. All are to be respected. All are to be freed up and protected from obstructions and ostracism; all have a purpose. All are a piece of God and, therefore, all are equal in the significance of their existence." Most importantly, all are to be treated accordingly.

The Circle

A woman aged and worn, well beyond her prime, enters our equation. Her children are all grown, doing well, independent, actively engaged in life. Her husband, her companion of more than fifty years, has left her to take his place in the magnificence of existence outside the boundaries of the Klein bottle. She stands alone, a brace on one foot, a cane in one hand, with sadness upon her face. She senses completion of her maternal and wifely duties. She senses the end drawing near and the desire to take the side of her life mate once more, the yearning to journey once again with her soul's companion. Her yearning to move on is accentuated by the weariness she already carries on her stooped shoulders, brought on by the knowledge of the vast quantities of energy she will have to muster and expend in order to start life over, alone.

Her emotions fall into the deep, dark, seemingly bottomless abyss of solitude, impatience, loneliness, memory, and despair over the energy needed to move to a new plateau in life, alone, on her own. She does not see her husband as he waits for her patiently, praying she will remain strong and patient in her resolve to follow her instincts to finish the marathon of life standing tall and proud of her accomplishments. She does not see her children as their thoughts frequently flash visuals of her standing tall and proud of them as adults, emitting emotions of encouragement to them as they face life's challenges, beckoning them to continue the journey through life as the rough spots arise.

Without even knowing it, she is a model to them, an object of hope, encouragement, strength, resolve, and faith. And so it is that she moves on through life, frequently toying with thoughts of what lies beyond, yet resisting the peace of the night due to the faith she has in the significance of her journey, a journey she does not understand.

Many have not been so fortunate as their models have lost hope and submitted to despair. Many models of joy have moved on to become models of sorrow and guilt, victimizing themselves through the ripple effect. The ripples undulate through eternity because they do not understand.

We leave the realm of committing violence to others and enter the realm of committing violence to ourselves. Life is a span of time composed of a myriad number of decisions regarding the path of life. Each action you choose to take is preceded by a multitude of forks in the road. As society becomes more and more technologically advanced, the number of forks emanating from each previous action become greater and greater.

Is it any wonder that we become increasingly unsure of ourselves, reeling more and more in the face of which road to take and which decision to commit to? Communication becomes instantaneous and the moral and ethical options appear to become more diverse. It's as if the world is spinning faster and faster and won't slow down. For more people, they just have to "get away from it all." They "need a vacation" and they don't want to take it at home, for home is not relaxing. It represents turmoil and decision making in the face of endless options.

People begin to see life as a constant struggle to maintain their gut feelings of right and wrong, their principles. Life becomes so fast paced, so many decisions to make with so many possibilities and repercussions, that rather than be enjoyable, life becomes a chore. Imagine that, life, a reality within a reality, becomes a chore. Wow, something is definitely wrong here. What's the solution? How do we regain control of our journeys and make them enjoyable, make them purposeful, claim them as our own once again?

The solution is simple yet difficult. You can only gain control of your life when you finally gain an understanding about what your purpose is in reality, when you finally understand your significance in eternity, when you finally understand where you fit into the puzzle of life. Once you understand this, you can logically allow your actions and behavior to transcend the concepts of "using others for my best interest" and raise your actions to the level of what's right. Once you are able to resolve the issue regarding your purpose, you can begin to control life rather than letting life control you.

It is conceivable that we will never know for certain what our purpose is in reality, what the purpose of reality itself is. This, however, is a negative hypothetical possibility. A hypothetical anything, especially a negative one, should never be the principle reason to stop searching, to stop striving, and to stop implementing perceived truths regarding our reality.

You may say, "It is ludicrous to search for perceived truths that we will never be able to prove and then live by them." This statement is one of hypocrisy. We do this all the time. Take as examples perceptions of religious truths and perceptions of existence itself. We have always taken the perceived concept of existence and used it as a source of hope, hope that we do exist, hope that we actually do have a purpose in reality. We have always taken perceived religious truths and used them as beacons to guide our behavior, as a light to follow regarding the effort we had to expend in order to orient our behavior at a higher level than other animals within our biosphere.

We take the perceptions of these truths and even though we cannot "prove" them, we live by our perception of them. Is taking the knowledge we have, using this knowledge to build a logical model of the purpose of reality, and then applying this universal philosophy to reinforce our present beliefs and satisfy our yearning to understand who we are, so illogical and unreasonable?

Such an extraordinary search, a search to find a logical purpose for ourselves, for reality, calls for finding an extraordinary answer. The answer must be simple, understandable, and able to be accepted by all. The answer must be complex enough to withstand the discoveries of future technologies and research. The answer must be flexible enough to bend but never break under the inevitable changes to come. The answer must be strong enough to become the third cornerstone for our principles.

Cornerstone 1: We exist.
Cornerstone 2: Faith and religions are guidelines for behavior within existence itself.
Cornerstone 3: Panentheism is a logical perception of ourselves strong enough to give credence to the behavioral guidelines provided by religion, faith itself.

These three cornerstones form the vertices of a triangle, which is one of the strongest geometric structures of "civil" engineering. Panentheism is the third cornerstone blooming oddly enough at the beginning of the third millennium, blooming as a rose, the rose of the mathematician Grandi. Just what does panentheism say that is simple yet complex, flexible yet unbreakable, minute yet contains such magnificent potential for both our present and future? Panentheism says:

God, a creator exists.
Reality exists.
Reality is in God.
Reality is a part of God.
Everything has a purpose.
Reality has a purpose.

We exist.
We are in reality.
We are in God.
We are a part of God.
Our souls, spirit, are pieces of God.
Our souls, spirit, have a purpose for existing in reality.
We deserve, have the right, and should demand, to be treated as God Itself.

You exist.
You are in reality.
You are in God.
You are a part of God.
Your soul is a piece of God.
You have a purpose for existing in reality.
You deserve, have the right, and should demand, to be treated as God.

These concepts lead to change in perception of self and of those around us. They lead to the understanding of principle, a concept that seems to have been left behind by yesterday's society, by today's society, and it appears, will be left behind by tomorrow's society.

What does this have to do with violence against oneself? Everything. The lack of understanding our purpose in reality, in eternity, makes it easier for us to compromise our principles. Lacking an understanding of our purpose in reality makes it difficult to use principles to guide our lives, for principles appear to have little significance when push comes to shove, when principles are needed most. But you may say, "I do have principles." You may have principles, but they are built upon two cornerstones: your perception of your existence and your perception of your faith.

These two cornerstones form two ends of a log floating upon the waters of reality. Standing upon the log of principle as we do is difficult. The log is wet, slippery, and rolls easily as it floats upon the dark waters of reality. There you stand upon the log, alone, trying to keep your balance, trying to keep from falling into the dark waters. It is easy to fall off even for the most principled of us.

Now, however, add a third cornerstone and one has constructed a triangle of three logs, a raft. The three endpoints of the triangular raft are perceptions of faith, perceptions of existence, perceptions of the understanding of our purpose within reality. These perceptions transform the rolling, slippery, wet log into a rigid stable platform, a raft to ride as we float upon the waters of reality. Stability at last to help us weather the rough seas to come, to help us overcome the temptation to compromise our principles that tie us together.

Without the understanding of any one of the three perceptions, we will be continually confronted with misunderstandings, conflict, and uncertainty regarding choices we must make in life. Without understanding our purpose in reality and the purpose of reality itself, we will continually compromise our principles through the process of submission and appeasement. These two actions reduce the very significance of each of us, and lead us to commit violence to our physical self, to our very essence, to the soul.

We have little understanding of our function in reality, our function of expanding God. We often compromise ourselves, our principles. There are two forms of compromising our status as God. Submitting to others is the process of being coerced into surrendering one's principles. Appeasing others is the process of buying off an aggressor at the sacrifice of one's principles. Submission and appeasement compromise one's very journey in reality. Submission and appeasement lead to committing violence against our very self, our very soul. If we do not accept our own significance, we cannot expect others to do so. Unless others perceive us to have significance, we cannot expect them to stop acting in a manner which benefits themselves at the expense of our personal journey.

We have to rely upon ourselves to take the first steps in the change of perceptions. We have to change our own perceptions of who we personally are. We have to understand and accept our own significance in reality. We have to recognize and respect our own journeys. Once we begin to respect our own personal journeys, we will begin to expect others to do the same.

Until we understand and accept that our own journey has significance equal to the journey of all others, we will continue to do violence to ourselves, we will continue to submit, we will continue to try to appease others. The place to start in terms of ourselves is learning to speak one of the most important words demanded of panentheistically oriented souls. The word is one of the shortest in the English language yet one of the most difficult to vocalize. The word is, "No."

No, I won't do that because it goes against my principles. No, I won't agree to that because it damages the principles of another person. No, I won't take on that task because I already have more than I can do. No, I won't subject myself to such overloads, abuse, humiliation, bigotry. No, I won't accept your abusive behavior. No, I will not continue to appease you or submit to your behavior. No, I refuse to continue to allow myself to be treated in this manner. No, I will not allow you or myself to treat me in that fashion anymore than I would subject God to such an abuse, to such humiliation, to such bigotry. I am a piece of God.

Your Essence

Two men, highly educated and seekers of truth, collaborate in writing the book, *The Bell Curve*. Two white men collaborate in order to dig out truth from the thick muck that lies beneath the dirty river of the unspeakable. Truth is hidden by the silt and polluted waters of racism. Some of the swirling silt is rich, fertile loam capable of producing understanding and growth. Some of the swirling silt is contaminated runoff from social misconceptions, bias, and the desire to subjugate and intimidate.

Two white men produce data that indicates some races are more intellectually adept than others. This data could be the beginning of understanding how physical development, social influence, and personal attitude affect intellectual development. Two white men conclude that their own Caucasian race is not the most intellectually capable but rather less capable than the Asian mind.

And what of their research? Is it taken at face value, recognized as being incomplete and just a beginning? No, the research is taken as a threatening and clumsy attempt of Caucasians to exploit African and Spanish Americans. The men are chastised and humiliated even by their own intellectual colleagues. The research is not recognized for what it is, a study in intellectual development in general, but rather as a judgmental piece of work aimed at the individual. No individual judgment was passed; no group judgment was passed. Everyone agrees that the individual is what matters and the individuals are all unique, nondescript from the statistics. It was the individual that took offense, however, because it was the individual that saw themselves as black or brown, clutching the misconception that the research proved one's individual skin color sentenced the individual to a specific mental capacity, not the brain itself. It was the individual that reeked violence upon itself through its own perception of what it believed its value in life was.

The question was never asked, "For whom did the 'Bell Curve' toll?" The question was never asked because it was just presumed that "'The Bell Curve' tolled for 'them.'"

You are not black! You are not female! You are not male! You are not mentally retarded! You are not homely! You are not homosexual! On and on it goes. You are none of these things. You are the soul. You are the essence within the machine. We perceive ourselves to be this or that but never what we truly are. We look in the mirror and see our outer packaging, but the mirror lies. The mirror only tells what the machine you occupy looks like and accentuates the perceived limitations your machine possesses. You take the image and embrace it as your own. The image is nothing but the exterior of the machine. It has nothing to do with you, your soul, with God.

You may perceive yourself to be limited by your machine, but you are relatively no more limited than any other. Your ability to contribute, to assist others, to create, to support a society intended to elevate the journey of all to equal status and advance our knowledge, understanding, experiences is no less than another. Your responsibility to find the means to do so, to demand the right to do so, to assist others to do so is not to be taken lightly, for your success at fulfilling this very responsibility will follow you into eternity itself through personal awareness. Personal awareness is nothing more than your creation of absolute reality out of God's very potentiality.

You may have had no input into what physical makeup your machine may take but you do have input into the manner in which you put your machine to work to accomplish its function in reality. You do have input into the accomplishments of your machine as it attempts to overcome the imperfections you perceive your machine to have. You may have had no input into the mental potential with which your machine may have shouldered your soul. You do, however, have the ability to decide how you are going to cope with that mental potential and to what degree you are going to implement that very potential in terms of how you treat yourself and how you voluntarily let others treat you.

You, your soul, must learn to deal with what tools it has to travel. You had no choice in terms of picking the machine of your soul, but you do have a choice regarding how you use that machine and when all is said and done, when your life's journey is over, your soul will be looking at its journey straight in the face in every detail. You, your soul, will be fully aware of every detail of its journey, of your journey and how it affected others, society, yourself, your soul, God.

Judgment is a primitive negative behavior still clinging to us and to society. Because we are shallow, because we judge others by the visual characteristics of their machines, we judge ourselves likewise. The lack of understanding of just who one is, one's essence, one's purpose in reality leads us to grasp for easy answers. And what easier answer can be found than what one sees in the mirror?

What are mirrors? They are what you use to view yourself. They sometimes are physical objects that reflect back an actual pictorial image. More often, mirrors are something else. They are people providing feedback through actions and verbalization. They are social parameters set up by others that cast judgmental labels. They are voices within yourself responding to people and society making judgmental determinates regarding our value as a person. Mirror images are values based upon what others casually see on a shallow level, not based upon the true person that lies within.

We let this happen. Not only do we voluntarily let society and people react to us based upon their shallow observations, but we also accept their judgments, ostracism, and rejection because we have no understanding of who we are and believe they must be right.

Our perception of ourselves as individuals needs to change. We need to elevate our perceptions of ourselves before we will demand that others treat us significantly. We can elevate our concepts of ourselves if we accept a universal philosophy that says all are of equal status through their very essence, the soul. Panentheism elevates all to a status above the machine, above the mind to the level of the essence of ourselves, the soul.

Panentheism says that all are equal since all are, in essence, their souls, and souls are a part of God. Since all are a portion of God, no one is better than another since nothing, at this point in our understanding of reality, is greater than or has more value than God, the Creator of reality itself. This revolutionary perception translates into the expectation and demand of respect from others as well as respect from yourself.

Charles Hartshorne was one of the first Western philosophers to provide a definitive analysis of panentheism. His efforts, if accepted by the general population, will not make some happy. It would mean the end of people using other people to elevate their own status. It would mean the end of "isms." It would mean the end of people allowing themselves to be used by others. It would mean the end of society tolerating people advancing themselves at the expense of others. It would mean the end of your allowing yourself to be abused.

The concept of a spouse tolerating their partner's physical or verbal abuse would no longer be acceptable in the eyes of the victim, for the victim would understand their function in reality and direction of their journey. A purpose of being abused and direction of toleration of such actions would lose all rationality within the mind of the oppressed for how could one subject themselves to these atrocious behaviors if one perceived themselves to be a part of God? How could you accept an abusive journey knowing that you would have to live with the consequences of the ripple effect caused by appeasement and submission?

Temporary submission to threats of physical violence and mental intimidation? Possibly. We must attempt to survive our reality, for we travel for a purpose, and to end that journey ends the ability we possess to accomplish that journey. Survival is an important responsibility we have to ourselves, others, society, and God. Continual submission to abusive and belittling actions, intimidation, physical violence, destruction of the environment, power plays, placement within status levels, racism, genderism, social stigmatisms, intellectual snubbing, sexual harassment, etc., are totally unimaginable if we accept the concept that we are a piece of God.

Submitting ourselves to abuse is unimaginable if we accept the concept that we are God. Tolerating such actions from people or society as they force actions and attitudes of these forms upon others would and should lead one to a state of absolute indignation and immediate active support of the one being abused. And just how do we go about showing our displeasure of such behavior? How do we show support of people being abused as we observe? How do we stop abusing ourselves or stop others from abusing us? Again, by saying, "No."

Panentheism supports three basic rights: the right to use the word "no;" the right to raise the importance of one's journey, God's journey, through reality to the level of all others; and the right to be treated with the respect extended by others to God.

If you accept the logic of panentheism, you accept the logic that you are God traveling in an isolated state from the portion of God outside reality. If you accept this simplistic concept, then you must logically accept that you are a portion of God. With this in mind, the next logical step is that you and I have the responsibilities for our own journeys and have the right to make judgmental decisions regarding our own journeys and how we want to proceed.

At this point, a disturbing questions surfaces. If our soul is a piece of God traveling reality in order to learn, create, and maintain societies that support this process, are we here to experience pain and despair? Looking back upon our history, we could conclude that enough pain and negative experiences have been generated to last for eternity. Looking at the present, enough tears are being shed to fill an ocean of time. Looking toward the future, we will never, within the foreseeable future, reach the level of sophistication to totally eliminate the tears of fear, humiliation, sadness, and pain which will continue to feed the torrential rivers of experiences leading to God's ocean of hurt.

A judgmental statement, yes, but any answer to the question would likewise be judgmental. So what's the point? The point is that you have free will as does everyone. You are traveling through this reality for a reason. You have the ability, the right, to make choices regarding your journey. We may not be able to completely stop the river of pain, sadness, hurt, subjugation, the demeaning of ourselves and others, but we can definitely reduce the flow of the river's tributaries. And what better tributary to start with than the tributary we create ourselves as we allow others to commit violence to our very own body and mind and thus to our very own soul? What better tributary to start with than the tributary we create as we commit violence to our own body and mind, our own soul? It is time to dry up the river of pain and sadness we generate as we abuse ourselves, as we allow others to abuse ourselves.

Understanding this freedom to make choices brings up the question, "What choice are you going to make for yourself?" Are you going to continue to allow others to lower your status to the level of an animal while they hold themselves up to be better than you? Are you going to allow others to use you based upon your surface appearances, your physical characteristics or your mental capacity, for their personal gain? Are you going to allow the journey of God, the journey for which you are responsible, to be subjected to a journey of despair and pain?

You are a portion of God. You are as valuable to the growth of God's very omnipotence, omniscience, omnipresence as anyone else. You will experience your own ripple effect throughout eternity with as much intensity as anyone else. You must take responsibility for your journey for it is more important to you than anyone else's journey; it is the only journey you have the right to control.

If panentheism is closer to being correct than pantheism or traditional theism, then there are three levels of empathy you will experience when you finish journeying this reality. You will experience the totality of God; you will experience the actions of others; you will experience the effects of your own actions. This third form of "experiencing" after your journey will be the most difficult to accept and endure. Experiencing the effects of your actions will, however, also be the most comforting, the most satisfying. The results of the actions or lack of actions we are responsible for in our journey through reality will be amplified a thousand times over through the knowledge that not only were we responsible for these actions, but we made the decision to act or not act under the autonomy of free will.

Where does this lead us? It leads us to the word "no." It leads us to taking responsibility for our own actions.

No, no, no, no, no!!! You may be my boss but, no, I will not take on that extra task. I have other obligations and I will not subject my journey to that type of stress. You may be my husband and I may be smaller than you but no, I will not keep coming back to your physical abuse or mental intimidation. My journey is as important as yours and I will, must, take responsibility for it. You may be a representative of authority and I may be black but I will not accept your treatment of me as an animal. My journey is too valuable to be influenced by the color of my skin. You may be socially correct in your sexual orientation and I may be homosexual but no,

I will not allow myself to be beaten into an inferiority complex. I have too much to contribute to society to let your concerns regarding the minor concept of my body's, my machine's, sexual leanings dominate my existence, my purpose in traveling reality.

There is no end to where we need to use the word "no." We cannot, as individuals however, be effective with the word "no" until we understand we have a purpose in reality as individuals. We cannot, as individuals, be effective in using the word "no" to protect our personal journeys from others until we accept our own importance, our own significance in reality. You cannot, as an individual, even effectively protect yourself from yourself until you have a personal understanding of what reality is and how you fit into it.

What could be more significant than believing, accepting, understanding that you are a portion of God? Your journey has a purpose and you have the responsibility to protect it from not only others but from yourself. You have the obligation and the right to attempt to stop the violence others are doing to you. You have the right and obligation to stop the violence you are doing to yourself. You have the free will, the choice, to say, "NO." Accepting your significance in reality will help you vocalize this short but difficult word. Understanding will help reinforce your faith in your true equal status with all others in society.

Understanding (logic) and faith (religion) will reinforce each other and double your conviction and determination to insist upon the concept of equality of all – equality brought on by the understanding of our essence, your essence, God Itself. Self violence and violence to others will gradually decline through the implementation of a universal philosophy, through an understanding and acceptance of your function in reality and the significance of reality itself.

The Glue

Women, rejected in their attempt to serve God, are put in their 'place' by the very social institution that preaches tolerance and acceptance. Women, in their desire to be compassionate, buckle to the strong arm techniques of history, submit to the greater power and accept the concept that males are on a higher plane than females, are closer to God than females. Women, not understanding that they in essence are not females but rather the soul itself, accept the proclamation of the 'superior males' and appease their male superiors through the act of submission. Will we never learn? Panentheism does not suggest that we accept subservience. It strongly suggests that we absolutely and vehemently reject subservience and appeasement. Panentheism insists upon acceptance of all for what they truly are – souls journeying.

A young woman yearning to reach up and touch the face of God is denied access to the most sacred level attainable by the soul itself and, instead, is only 'allowed' to reach up and touch the face of a man that has touched the face of God. If women are souls journeying reality within the confines of a female machine, then why should that soul be denied the same access, the same proximity to God that the soul within a male machine is allowed to attain? Women should never allow society, social institutions, to subjugate them in such a humiliating fashion.

But just as women should never tolerate their being denied the most revered position of proximity to God, the position of priesthood, so they must as well never tolerate others being denied the same opportunity just because it would seem to cancel out the sins of the fathers before them. No soul can rightfully be burdened with the sins of their father, for each soul is unique and comes from God.

Violence to others and violence to oneself are two forms of violence that have no place in our journey. And just what holds all this violence together? Society does. Society acts as a cementing agent that glues the two halves of violence, violence to others and violence to oneself, together. But let's explore society to see just what this means.

We all know violence exists. We all see it, read about it and feel it. It does not need graphics or statistics to be verified. Violence to others exists to such a large degree in our society because we tolerate it and look the other way. We give it a token acknowledgment with fragmented, uncoordinated efforts and then move on with our lives.

In this section, we will just take a small sampling of the multitude of various forms of physical violence that we allow to exist within the environment in which our present state of existence journeys. We create this environment through quiet approval and passive acceptance.

When you and I both no longer want to take the effort or feel we are capable of resolving social problems, we create social entities to do it for us. As these social institutions grow in power and size, they take on an identity of their own. Through time, they gain characteristics of the overall society which created them. If the society that creates them is filled with apathy, they eventually become filled with apathy. If the society that creates them is filled with self righteousness, they become filled with self righteousness. If society is filled with color, gender, economic, intellectual, self serving biases, the social institutions become images of these very values.

If we do not understand who we are, what our purpose in reality is, and for that matter, what reality itself is, how can we expect our social institutions to rise above the level of their creators? How can we expect them to understand that their purpose is to aid us in our journey through reality? When we use others to advance our own purposes, how can we expect social entities, which are created by us, to do any differently, for just as God created us in Its own image, so we create social institutions in our own image.

The difference is that our creation, social institutions, are not provided free will but rather are given directives. Social institutions are not created to solve problems but to alleviate them. What is the difference? When we create an institution, it takes on our image. Social institutions take on an undertone of self preservation. They thrive in their directive to alleviate problems, but they will not extend themselves to the point of attempting to eliminate the problem, for that would be an action of self annihilation.

As our social institutions grow, they also become more adept and subtle in their skills regarding their ability at self preservation. A prime example is the institution of social welfare. After spending over five trillion dollars to eliminate poverty in the U.S., it has been estimated that we have made no net impact in terms of eliminating the problem. In other words, the institutions created to eliminate poverty have grown and have honed their ability to protect themselves, to protect their turf, to assure the continuation of the problem for which they were created.

Just how do these institutions manage to promote the continuation of the problems they were created to eliminate? They do so through subtle and sometimes bold actions of violence directed at us, souls, God. They do so through interfering with the journeys of the very people they were created to assist. We can look at the result in terms of the negative and say, "How awful." Or we can look at this and say, "How interesting that social institutions take on one of the primary characteristics of people, the characteristic of self preservation." If we take the later tact, we can learn from the situation and begin to eliminate the characteristic of self preservation we build into our creation of social institutions.

In place of self preservation, we need to consciously build into the appropriate social institutions the desire, motive, and directive of self annihilation. Self annihilation would be achieved through the successful accomplishment of the task these social institutions were given to perform, such as poverty elimination.

How can I say that "we" allow this to happen? I can say "we" because you and I have known about the continual violence generated by social institutions for a long time, ever since we have stepped out of childhood and into the realm of being able to take charge of our own journey. Once we accept our independence from our parents, we must accept responsibility for the makeup of our environment, including any apathetic social aspect of the reality within which we must travel.

Identifying the problem of physical violence to others is not enough. We all know the problem exists. When we point a finger and say, "There is an example of physical violence that is not tolerable," we must take the responsibility of presenting a viable solution to the problem. The solutions may not always work but at least we initiate the process by suggesting possibilities.

Changing our perceptions is the first step. We must start seeing others as equals. We must start recognizing the body and mind of others as the mechanism of travel for the soul. We must recognize that each soul is a portion of God. With this in mind, we will have no option but to attempt to protect the journey of God, of all individuals, for those journeys are in essence our journey since we, too, are God and we all will merge once again into the greater entity of God. If we can establish panentheism as a foundation for our actions and faiths, then the rest is easy for it becomes obvious what our actions must become.

To begin recognizing problems and creating solutions, identify who you are and what your purpose is in reality – a universal philosophy, identify the problems that exist around you and develop viable solutions regarding them, and work to implement solutions. If we do not find examples of intrusions upon individual journeys in our own home, we have but to walk out the front door and look up and down the street. More deaths, mutilations, sexual abuse, enslavement, and intimidation goes on behind the doors of the "home" than anywhere else in society. In this situation, we are going to focus on men, but men aren't the only ones committing the atrocities. Who is committing atrocities is not the point here. The point is that when the atrocity is being committed, it is being directed at someone, some soul. This is where we need to direct our attention. We need to stop focusing on the perpetrator and start focusing on the victim. With this in mind, we begin to seek solutions for the victim, the one being abused, the one whose journey is being violated.

To illustrate a possible solution to a frequent, abusive, dangerous situation, let's look at the problem of spousal abuse, wife beating in particular. The abuse may be the result of past child abuse, social pressures, alcohol, drugs, vile tempers or lack of self control on the part of the husband. The reason, the cause, is not the point. The point is that it happens and when it does, the victim needs assistance. Society has found a means of helping the victim in centers known as "safe homes." Society has shirked its responsibilities, however, since it has not put its financial resources and manpower behind such solutions.

If society and individuals recognized people in society as vehicles transporting portions of God, they would see that supporting concepts such as "safe homes" must be done so financially and with the necessary professional and volunteer manpower. This would not be a case of being a "do gooder," but would rather be a fulfillment of our responsibility.

One could argue that we already have "safe homes." We do have some small centers in some cities for people in need; however, we do *not* have nearly enough of them. If they were truly an established, accepted part of society, they would be well-known, well-funded, and within easy access to all people who need them. They would become an integral part of our society and educational systems. They would always have room for one more person. They would be staffed by professionals 24 hours a day. They would be learning centers to train and educate battered people regarding how to free their souls for a more independent journey in reality.

The centers would rise above the concept of identification with battered spouses to identification with battered people: abused children, stalking victims, assault victims, the intimidated, the vulnerable. They would be large centers built near police quarters, social workers, social assistance offices, clinics, human resources for religious needs, social and self help groups such as Alanon, drug rehab, AA, teen pregnancy homes, and on and on. They would have satellite homes and connections in every city, neighborhood, school, block club, PTA, and church. They would be perceived and supported as proud accomplishments and monuments of society rather than the present centers that are under-funded, existing in just a very small number of cities.

The question becomes one of manpower. How can we question manpower when full unemployment is never reached? Everyone in society is needed to improve society. No one should be allowed to stand idle day after day. No one should be paid to be unemployed. "Safe homes" would no longer be in subtle, obscure locations that only the fortunate are aware of. They would become mega-safe havens for those in need. They would be complexes with satellites placed throughout society as highly visible, professionally and voluntarily staffed resources for physically, mentally, spiritually violated individuals.

At the same time as establishing these resources for souls in society whose journeys are being violated, we would, with the new found perception of ourselves, see the formation of such highly visible resources as monuments of pride. Not pride in the fact that we need them, but rather pride in the fact that we recognized our shortcomings as humans and took the time, money, and effort to establish a means to overcome the intrusions we have allowed our fellow souls to suffer. It would be a statement of our intent to not let it happen again in the future. It would be a statement of our intent to recognize all souls as equal to our own soul.

Are there not enough positions to fill with educated, trained people? There are presently not enough funded positions in these social service centers; however, there is so much to do when we view ourselves and others as portions of God that the positions to be filled by trained educated personnel is almost limitless. The amount of manpower needed is so phenomenal that no one needs to be placed in a meaningless job; no one needs to be left without a task to complete. There is room for all, from the independently mobile to the quadriplegic, from the strong to the bedridden, from the genius to the mentally impaired. We tolerate such waste in society regarding the potential of so many when so much needs to be done.

We certainly need social institutions. They are the means of coordinating the "thousand points of light," which are made up of blacks, college grads, social isolates, whites, intellectuals, firemen, athletes, women, men, children, physically and mentally challenged, teachers, hippies, nerds, homosexuals, factory workers. And what can they do? They can communicate via phone calls, letters, notes, visits, education, encouragement, mentoring, counseling, listening to others and on and on.

The concept sounds like an encroachment of more governmental power over the people. It need not be. The centers already have their nucleuses formed and built in our society. They just need to become a coordinated effort that takes on a slightly different approach involving a bigger picture. The present nucleus and satellites now in place are hospitals, police stations, churches, schools, self help groups, community centers, government buildings, courts, etc., all acting in an isolated fragmented manner. They need to begin working in a coordinated fashion.

How is this different from what we have now? Under the new perception of all people being a portion of God, all the present satellites would become, by necessity, tied into each other in order to maximize their potential. They would become cooperating entities with one sole purpose – preventing the intrusion upon the independent journey of all souls. The primary purpose of each institution would be to free up each soul to journey in an unobstructed manner to accomplish its purpose in life.

Recognition of who we are as individuals and as a species would give us the big picture needed to place all these fragmented resources together as a unit. The primary goal of the fragmented units would be to unite as one organization to protect the journeys of all individuals. Their purpose would not be to define that journey, nor to judge that journey, but rather to protect that journey. They would be there to assist individuals, provide options, and provide safe havens and resting places. They would never be able to define or judge that journey for that would be just another form of interference.

The goal is the elimination of violence created by social institutions through the elimination of self preservation unwittingly infused into these very institutions we created. We can eliminate social violence, the cement we have created bonding the two halves, violence to one's self and violence to others. We can eliminate social institutions perpetuating the violence they are created to destroy.

By accepting panentheism, we would have a new perception of ourselves, the image that we are none other than a portion of God. Society and social institutions are our creation and, as such, take on our very image. Therefore, as we change our perceptions of who we are, social institutions will change. As we raise our perceptions of who we are to the new heights we never before dared dream of, our society and social institutions will follow, for they are nothing but the reflection of humankind.

Points

A sixty-year-old man of the "cloth" stands stooped and despondent. A man who has reached out and touched the face of God is forced to look back and face his action in life even before he steps into the reality of his next journey. The man is draped symbolically in black as he faces traumatized young men he has touched in his desire to fulfill his physical yearnings.

A social institution has spawned a quadruple tragedy. A man who has reached out and touched God, the very essence of his origination, has violated himself physically by bringing down the wrath of society upon himself. Secondly, he has violated himself mentally by bringing mental despair upon his own perceptions regarding the contributions his years of journeying has left within reality. Next, he has violated his own environment by creating for himself a permanent cocoon of social rejection and loathing. Last and saddest of all, he has violated himself spiritually by violating others, thereby creating ripples he will experience throughout eternity.

All four forms of violation have occurred because the man of the cloth never understood, he never was able to logically reason through his significance in reality, he was never able to sort out the contradictions because logic was not acceptable as part of the thought process. All behavior had to be based upon faith alone.

We begin to see the difference between the success of mathematics, which accepts logic as a companion, and the failure of morality, which rejects logic as a companion to religion. Why the difference in the success rate of the two? Geometry deals with what we can see. Morality deals with what we feel. Is what we see more reliable in describing our reality than what we feel inside? Is not what we feel more important than what we see?

If you had to choose, would you choose being blind while at the same time feeling good about life, about yourself, about others, about your accomplishments in life, about having lived life, about facing death or would you choose being able to see while at the same time feeling depressed about life, about yourself, about others, about your accomplishments in life, about having lived life, about facing death? Geometry may be built upon the foundation of nothingness, but that foundation incorporates one of our senses, a universal physical sense – vision. Sight gives geometry the foundation it needs to be a successful, universally accepted concept.

We can change the success rate of morality. The problem is that morality has nothing incorporated within its foundation that acts as a universal sense. The solution, therefore, is simple. We must add a universal sense to morality, the universal sense of logic. We must make morality understandable logically to the common person, to society. We must create, through rationality, a universal philosophy that is as indisputable to morality as geometry is to mathematics. If we do this, and we can do this, we will create a foundation of logic so successful that all areas of morality and religion will use it as an absolute, a foundation justifying their existence.

Is there a logical basis for morality? Is there a logical solution to accepting not only the behaviors of others that do not conform to our own, but to accepting the individuals themselves whose behavior, beliefs, and principles differ from ours? Can we find the logic that will allow us to accept cultures that are drastically different from our own, to respect their cultures, beliefs, and principles while at the same time maintaining our own principles, traditions, and beliefs?

This unique logic might better be called a universal philosophy. How do we create a universal philosophy that would elevate our perception of ourselves and others to such an extent that, if truly accepted, the thought of abusing ourselves, others, society or the environment becomes unthinkable? Wouldn't creating such a philosophy be a horrendous task? In actuality, the creation of such a philosophy should be quite simple since the philosophy itself, by definition, needs to be simple. In fact, the seed of the philosophy already exists and has been planted. It is just waiting to germinate and flourish. It is just waiting for us to water it, nurture it, and shape it. The seed is panentheism:

1. Reality exists.
2. We, you and I, exist within reality.

3. Reality had a beginning.
4. The beginning was initiated by a creative force.
5. Reality exists within the force that created reality.
6. Reality coexists with its creative force for a reason.
7. Reality depends on its creative force for continuation.
8. The creative force depends upon the reality it created as a place to travel, to learn, to create, to expand upon its omnipotence, omnipresence, and omniscience.
9. The creative force travels reality in many forms, one of which is within you as the soul.
10. You are a piece of God and deserve, must demand, to be treated with the appropriate respect as you travel reality, life.
11. Everyone is a piece of God and deserves, must demand, to be treated with the appropriate respect as they travel reality.
12. You must treat everyone with the appropriate respect as they travel reality for they are a piece of God.
13. You must demand everyone around you be treated with appropriate respect as they travel reality.
14. You will return from whence you came carrying with you the results of your travels.
15. You will experience for eternity the pleasant warmth or painful fire of the knowledge and worse yet, the full empathy, of the direct and indirect results of your travels through reality or what is called the ripple effect of your life.

This simple philosophy is mind shattering in its potential impact regarding our behavior within reality. With this universal philosophy, the status of all people would be elevated to the level of God, a level so high that we would never dare use another for our own personal benefit. We would no longer casually allow ourselves to be used or abused for we would perceive ourselves to be God. Misuse of the environment? Unthinkable! The environment is a place for God to travel. The environment depleted of its cleanliness and resources, left barren for the travels of future generations, future journey's of God? Ludicrous! Social institutions running amok, abusing individuals, pieces of God Itself? Blasphemous! Social institutions perceiving themselves as having a life of their own as important as individuals, pieces of God? Unimaginable!

How is this different than what we have presently? Without panentheism and only our historical, moral perceptions in place, the status of all people vary and is used as rationale for our behavior of using others to benefit ourselves. We feel we are beneath God, some more so than others. Survival of the fittest. Watch out for yourself. Never turn your back. Climb the ladder to "success" by stepping on the careers of others. An animalistic society of crime, poverty, abuse, depression, immorality. The sad thing is we cannot even agree what "immorality" is!

We casually allow ourselves to be used or abused to gain what we perceive to be success, safety, protection, security, and punishment for wrongs we must have committed. We constantly return to spousal abuse, life on the street, sexual harassment, racial slurs, ostracism from the house of God, demeaning reprimands, etc.

We perceive the environment as a place to be used for the expediency of the present, a place that we use for our own benefit, a place we will no longer experience in another hundred years or so. Why not make the most of it now and forget the future generations? The future generations are just "people." They are no more important than I am, so they can think about themselves when they get here. Is the environment a place to travel? Hardly! The environment is a place used and depleted of its cleanliness and resources, left barren for the travels of future generations, if that's what it takes to advance.

We allow social institutions to run amok, abusing individuals, and think, "So what?" I am an administrator of this institution and advancing its power advances my level of authority and power. This raises my self esteem, which is good for me. It is what I want. Everyone else is getting theirs; I want my piece of the pie. Social institutions perceiving themselves as having a life of their own, in essence as important as individuals? Certainly, doesn't this institution try to benefit people? So what if a few are emotionally destroyed in the process. Overall, we do more "good" than "bad" for people.

There you have the essence. Society with panentheism and society without panentheism. Your choice, my choice, our choice – to accept panentheism or not. We can keep the distress of what we have and continue to perpetuate our present society in all its misery. Or we can accept a new foundation for faiths, a new perception of ourselves which will elevate ourselves to the very level of God.

We can continue our present mode of function within a reality we have left undefined as to its purpose, our purpose. It is a state of being defined by confusion and uncertainty. This is a state of being which has historically always lead to collapse. Or we can define our reality as having a specific purpose and define ourselves as having a specific purpose. We can define ourselves in terms of a higher plane of existence, a process that would lead to a whole new perspective of who we are, who those around us are, and even what our environment is.

Acceptance of a panentheistic view is a radical shift in philosophy. We would have only been able to implement this radical change in the past through the means of major violence, cultural collapse or global war. Panentheism is a radically different way of looking at humankind, a revolutionary change in perception. It is a perception that can be generated for the first time in a peaceful manner. Panentheism is a new philosophical foundation for faith that would not destroy faith, but would only strengthen the need for individuality and uniqueness.

Panentheism is simple in concept, yet radical concerning perceptual views of oneself, others, the environment, and social institutions. Can we accept it? If we want to; it is our choice. It is our decision, yours and mine.

It's Time

We come full circle. We return to where we started. We return to the issue of life and death. A man of education, a man of prominence, acting as the designated spokesman for 100 independently owned abortion clinics, admits providing false testimony to committees of the most powerful governmental body in the world. The executive director of the National Coalition of Abortion Providers admits testifying to a U.S. Congressional Committee about the rarity of partial birth abortion.

The deliberating body hears the words "only 500 are performed a year" and with the prodding of pro-choice organizations, editorial staffs involving all forms of news media, and political organizations hoping to reap the benefits of headline grabbing events, the President decides the number is acceptable and vetoes the ban on partial birth abortion.

No one wants to take responsibility for the action when the number turns out to be five thousand or more deaths of viable babies per year. The Republicans blame the Democrats, the pro-life organizations blame the pro-choice organizations, the President blames the man who testifies, the man who testifies blames his fear of damaging the pro-choice movement, and the editors of the news media sit back in a "holier than thou" position and blame everyone but themselves.

And what of the babies? No one mentions the babies! No one understands that these were not just babies; they were young souls about to travel reality in order expand upon the very omniscience, omnipotence, omnipresence of God. No one understands that the number 500 or 5,000 is not what is important. What is important is the soul itself, each soul. No one understands that an atrocity is an atrocity whether it be committed one time or a thousand times. Right is right and wrong is wrong.

We have to begin to look at things differently! We cannot go on as irresponsible adolescents. We either grow up through our own choice to do so or we will be forced into taking a break through collapse. It's time to grow up and take on the responsibilities that goes with the position our place in reality requires. It's time we recognize who we are as individuals and as entities in reality and accept the responsibilities that go along with that realization.

And just who is it that we are? We are a piece God. We are not God; we are a piece of God and that is significantly different. We do not have the total power, the total knowledge or the total expansiveness of the Creator of our reality. We do, however, have some of all of these characteristics as individuals and even more so as a species. We are, as individuals and a species, in our late adolescence acting as children but thinking we are grown up, having great potential but not yet utilizing it, wanting to continue as we are, irresponsible, but wanting the privileges that go along with maturity.

We refuse to look at what we know in order to define our place in reality because we fear the burden it would place upon us in terms of acting responsibly. Those in charge, those in our society with power generated by the excitement, enthusiasm, and irrationality of adolescent thought and peer pressure, do not want us to grow up and act responsibly. If we would do so, those in power would lose their status of being power brokers, a status they find to be exhilarating and inflating.

Think about it. If we all started thinking independently, with the understanding that we as well as all others were actually God Itself, what would that do to the authoritative position of power brokers in society? What would that do to our expectation of the responsibility of people in power? What would that do to the actual concept of "power" itself? Our whole concept of leadership would change! This would compel and require us to quickly, efficiently, and authoritatively replace leaders that were using power as a self serving tool.

We would pick leaders who recognize individuals as pieces of God on a journey with purpose. The role of power broker would change to a role of facilitator. The responsibilities of the people in power would transform into a position of facilitating the journeys of all people, of all life. This would transform a position of leadership and power from one of consolidating power and expanding one's authority, to facilitating journeys equally for all individuals.

All journeys are of equal importance when looked at as being journeys of God.

Who are these power brokers? They are the upper echelon of religious institutions, political organizations, government, crime syndicates, massive corporations, mass media, etc. Can you imagine any of these leaders saying, "You are just as important as I am. Your journey deserves as much recognition and consideration as mine. I am here to accommodate your journey as well as my own. My purpose in filling this position of leadership is not to accommodate my personal journey only but to provide equally for your journey as well."

Now slide down the social ladder to what we call the "bottom." As you slide down the social ladder (built by ourselves, not God), stop frequently and get off at different levels. Apply the same questions at these different levels to generals, mayors, administrators, foreman, husbands, wives, ex-wives, ex-husbands, mothers, fathers, in-laws. Do any of them want to give up the power, authority, and control they have over others? Will this ever occur? Probably not, because we have an outdated understanding of who we are. In actuality, you could say we have no understanding of who we are. We perceive ourselves to be "people" and when you ask what that means, no one can give you an answer of significance.

Can our society change dramatically? Can we change so comprehensively that our whole outlook regarding life, individuals, religion, society, the environment, and even ourselves would undergo a revolutionary change so immense it would compare to the agricultural, industrial, and technological revolutions? Change of this degree has seldom occurred in our perception of ourselves and when it did, it was breathtaking. Each change of this magnitude was generated by a simple change in our philosophical perception of our place within reality. Both realities, the "physical" one we occupy and perceive with the senses and the "spiritual" reality from which we inherently sense we came and to which we will return, must have simple perceptions changed in unison for revolutionary change to occur. The vehicle for change must be simple enough in nature for all to understand yet broad enough to touch upon all aspects of life from the religious to the social, from the global to the everyday action of the individual, from the historical to the future. Panentheism could effect such a change.

Panentheism has been around for some time but hasn't been universally accepted because of logic. Just how could we be God and behave as we do? Why would God put Itself through the wringer of life we go through? If we are a piece of God, why don't we change things? Why would we treat each other like we do? What possible purpose could there be for us to exist as we are?

Previously, no answers could logically be constructed to satisfactorily rationalize solutions to these questions. We couldn't rationalize panentheistic concepts because we were looking in the wrong places. We were looking for the wrong things as we attempted to find the answer to our purpose in reality. We had no idea what to look for or where to look. We were treading on virgin territory. Never before had we attempted to use the scientific process of model building through the consolidation of all our basic knowledge to provide rationality and universality to the questions, "Who am I? Who are people? What is our purpose in reality?"

We were able to tread on the brink of understanding but we could never bridge the gap to the other side because the bridge we had to cross was not built yet. The components of the bridge were composed of our knowledge, scattered throughout history, fragmented and scattered through the cultures of our world. This knowledge was kept apart by the conflicts and self preservation instincts of the spheres of our society ranging from the scientific, religious, governmental, social, to the philosophical.

Panentheism is a concept that could pervade all of society without destroying any part of it. It is a perception of reality capable of radically altering all aspects of our social orders as well as our moral and individual perceptions. Panentheism is a simple concept embracing the idea that God, the Creator of reality, can grow in omnipotence and you and I are the means It uses to do so. This simple idea could initiate an avalanche of change.

Although panentheism is a simple perceptual change, it turns out to be a radical change in our perception of ourselves and our function in reality as well as how we understand and solve violence and conflict. Radical change begets radical change. Panentheism would create radical change for a better, stronger, more compassionate, humane future.

All that we, you and I, have to do to start the process is choose to do so.

"The philosophers have only interpreted the world in various ways. The point however, is to change it."

Theses on Feuerbach, 1888

Daniel J. Shepard, author of *You & I Together*, earned a B.S. Degree from the University of Michigan and a Master's Degree in Physical Science from Eastern Michigan University. He currently teaches school in Livonia, Michigan. *In the Image of God* is his second book and he is presently writing his third.

To order or to correspond with Daniel J. Shepard, write to:

W.E. Hope, Inc.
118 Main Center, Suite 226
Northville, Michigan 48167
(810) 349–1317

www.wehope.com